Slug Tossing

and Other
Adventures of a Reluctant Gardener

Slug Tossing

and Other
Adventures of a Reluctant Gardener

Meg DesCamp

SASQUATCH BOOKS
SEATTLE

To Kevin: More Today . . .

Printed in the United States of America.
Distributed in Canada by Raincoast Books Ltd.
02 01 00 99 98   5 4 3 2

Cover design: Karen Schober
Cover and interior illustrations: Susannah Bettag
Interior design and composition: Kate Basart

DesCamp, Meg.
        Slug tossing and other adventures of a reluctant gardener /
    Meg DesCamp.
        ISBN 1-57061-044-4
        1. Gardening—Oregon—Portland—Anecdotes. 2. Gardeners—
    Oregon—Portland—Anecdotes. 3. DesCamp, Meg. I. Title.
        SB455.D47   1998
        635'.092—dc21   97-44117

Sasquatch Books
615 Second Avenue
Seattle, Washington 98104
(206) 467-4300
books@sasquatchbooks.com
http://www.sasquatchbooks.com

Sasquatch Books publishes high-quality adult nonfiction and children's books related to the Northwest (Alaska to San Francisco). For more information about our titles, contact us at the address above, or view our site on the World Wide Web.

Contents

Chapter 1

Southeast Alder Street, Portland, Oregon

"Absolutely not." I glared first at Kevin, then out the window of our car at the small blue house across the street. A For Sale sign rode hopefully on the weed-choked front lawn.

"You won't even get out and look?" asked my husband.

"No! It's a piece!" I held up my hand and began counting on my fingers. "The roof is falling off. The yard looks awful. I hate that rock garden in the front bank. The trim is peeling and the house is too small." The fingers on my left hand were used up, and I stopped to draw a breath.

"Actually, I think the rock garden is sort of pretty," Kevin said calmly. "And besides, you have to cut the owners some slack on the way the house looks. It's not even officially on the market until later this week. You heard the real estate agent say they were going to replace the roof and paint the trim, didn't you?"

"Real estate agents will say anything." I glared again, this time straight ahead, arms folded.

"Okay. Well, I want to look at it. I won't be long." Kevin got out, closed the car door carefully, and walked up the sloping driveway. I watched as a man carrying a push broom came out of the small white garage. They talked. The man gestured toward our car. Kevin shook his head.

Meanwhile, I fumed. After living in San Francisco for two years, we'd moved back to Portland, Oregon, and had been looking at houses for six months. The real estate boom was in full force, and we were feeling its effect. We'd slogged through countless Portland winter downpours and spring drizzles without finding a house that fit our criteria: old and interesting, in a stable urban neighborhood, reasonably priced, with space inside for my home office and outside for hanging out on summer evenings. We also wanted room for a few flowers and vegetables—nothing serious, just some plants here and there.

"How about the westside suburbs?" Kevin had asked me once during the course of our home search.

"Not with this wife," I'd replied.

"Okay. I'd rather be in town, too. Shorter commute for me."

We hadn't discussed the 'burbs again.

It was now July. We'd reached the end of our rope. We'd almost reached the end of suitable neighborhoods, as well. The real estate agent called this particular area transitional. I called it marginal.

"I should know," I'd reminded Kevin as we drove over to look at the little blue house. Several years earlier, I had lived in this neighborhood for a few months and sworn I would never return. Too much litter on the sidewalk. Too few owner-occupied homes. Too many weeds, rusty cars, taverns on the busy street a few blocks over. The neighborhood had a high riff-raff factor, and I clearly remembered my too frequent encounters with stumbling drunks and glowering druggies. I did not want to share home base with them again.

Sure, there was an eighty-acre park two blocks north of the little blue house, and a trendy shopping district eight blocks south. But the negatives, I declared loudly and repeatedly, outweighed the positives.

"Things have changed," the real estate agent said

Right.

Now, I sat in the car, sending poisonous glances at my beloved husband's back and wishing I'd stayed in the Midwest where I was raised so we wouldn't be fighting over this stupid house. Then I realized that if I'd stayed in the Midwest, I wouldn't have this particular husband to fight with—this funny, smart, cute husband. Besides, I hadn't given my Michigan hometown a single backward glance on the day I left. It was too small, too cold, too . . . Midwestern.

Spring in the town where I grew up was chilly—sometimes downright cold—but that never stopped my mom.

"Meggie? I've bought you some lettuce seeds. Would you like to plant a vegetable garden this year?" Mom stood in the garage with a hopeful look on her face and seed packets in her hand.

Nice try, Mom, I thought, as I continued to shoot baskets in our driveway. Why should I crawl around on my hands and knees in the dirt when there was a farmer's market six blocks away that had enough lettuce to feed the entire county?

I was thirteen years old when Mom tried to entice me into growing my own vegetable patch in our large Michigan backyard. By then, she should have known better. In seasons past, it had been pansies—"Aren't their little faces just like kittens?"—and houseplants—"Look at these pretty African violets. Would you like to have the pink one or the purple one?"

It was hopeless. Rather, *I* was hopeless. For years, it had been obvious the family green thumb had passed me by. *What was the point?* I wondered each time Mom coerced me into planting pansies and pulling weeds. At thirteen, watching developing plant life seemed like the ultimate waste of time. I was interested in developing just two things: larger breasts and a better shot from the free-throw line.

My apparent lack of the gardening gene may have been due to the fact that I was the only member of our family not born in the fertile Pacific Northwest. Or perhaps it was because, as the youngest of eight kids, I just didn't want to do what everyone else was so good at. My mother faithfully planted bulbs in the fall and annuals in the spring; my brothers and sisters grew hordes of aggressively healthy houseplants at home and in their college dorm rooms. Dad was in charge of the pruning. He had worked in the Pacific Northwest forests as a college student and now ran a pulp mill, so he knew something about trees and shrubs and how they grow. But the closest I got to the earth was throwing mud balls at other kids in the neighborhood.

Gardening just seemed like a lot of hard work with highly uncertain results. Every year, Mom bemoaned the harsh Michigan climate, so unlike the Pacific Northwest. Our soil was dense and unforgiving. We regularly lost plants to long stretches of subzero winter weather. I couldn't see the charm in irises or gladiolus or peonies, and roses, I thought, were highly overrated. The only part of the garden I liked was the two long, lush lilac hedges, whose fragrant purple blooms always accompanied my late May birthday.

While I grew up amid Midwestern mores and weather, my brothers and sisters fled Michigan to return to their native Pacific Northwest; they all settled in Portland. My parents made it clear that they would return to the West Coast when Dad retired. But I concentrated on life in our small Lake Michigan town. Summer days were spent at the beach, winter nights skiing or skating. Autumn was crisp and clear and colorful, full of football games and marching band practice. Each spring was well earned after months of snow and cold. The shores of Lake Michigan were, I thought, a great place to live.

Even so, the family pull toward the West Coast proved strong. After trips "home" I would moon over the photography books we'd brought back—books with names like *Oregon* and *The Cascades*. Each page revived a sharp memory of spectacular beauty. Each visit made it harder to consider living in Michigan forever.

As I went through college, I began to seriously consider the advantages of living in a mild climate. A Christmas trip to Portland when I was twenty-one settled any doubt. For an entire week, I was astounded. I could actually go outside without wearing six layers of clothing. Flowers bloomed. Plants were green and lively, not buried under mounds of snow and slush. A trip to the ocean included a chance to hike in the coastal mountains, a far cry from fighting thigh-high snow to walk Lake Michigan's frozen shores.

It was sixty-five degrees when I boarded the plane to return to school. Four hours later, I descended into a Michigan blizzard. That did it. I dumped my boyfriend and began making serious plans to move. One year later, I had my college degree and was in a car heading west.

What I found, besides seemingly endless rain ("Think of it as liquid sunshine," urged a would-be boyfriend, whose calls I immediately quit returning) and an economic recession that made hash of my under-graduate English degree, was an overabundance of plants and the people who encourage them.

"Gee, here's a great idea," I said sarcastically, reading aloud from a gar-dening column in the *Oregonian*. " 'Now that we have extended light in the evenings, put that extra time to good use by pulling weeds or checking your roses for aphids.' " I snorted and took another sip of tea. "What sort of idiot would waste a perfectly good summer evening working in the garden when you could be out on a bike ride instead?"

"Idiots like your sisters," my sister Therese responded tartly. Elizabeth just rolled her eyes.

As an underemployed recent college graduate, I was grateful to be sharing an old, rundown house that my sisters had recently purchased in Portland's rapidly gentrifying Northwest neighborhood. But I did not understand their fascination with plants.

I helped out enthusiastically with the home's renovation. We painted, and plumbed, and pulled up layer after layer of rotten flooring in our bit for urban renewal. We regularly called our oldest sister, Jeanne, who was raising a family in Wisconsin, and regaled her in chorus with stories of dry rot and mice and men. And we got on with our professional lives—Elizabeth running a low-cost home-building program, Therese working as a lobbyist for a social services agency, and me floundering around in the communications industry as an advertising copywriter, publishing sales representative, radio sales rep—whatever paid the bills.

After the inside of the house was livable, my sisters took their efforts outside. Elizabeth was fairly restrained, concentrating on making a compact, efficient vegetable patch with some decorative touches. Therese, however, was out of control.

Therese would plant anything, and she would plant it anywhere. She spent the entire spring and summer digging smelly, evil-looking brown stuff into the front yard and sticking flowers into every available patch of bare dirt. Huge clay pots filled with huger, unidentifiable green things took over the large, sagging front porch.

Finally, she went too far. One weekend she excavated a circle of grass from the front lawn; in its place sprouted an enormous, and enormously ugly, rhubarb plant.

"Rhubarb in the front yard?" Elizabeth asked, not too calmly, when she spotted it.

"Relax. You want rhubarb pie, don't you?" Therese finished patting dirt around the plant's roots.

"What, you can't buy the stalks at the store anymore?" I put in from the front porch, where I was trying out a battered lounge chair and reading a murder mystery.

Therese glared at me. I shrugged. Elizabeth threw her hands in the air and retreated to her backyard veggie patch.

One week later, the rhubarb plant was convincingly dead, its enormous, heart-shaped leaves drooping in the summer heat.

That did it. We surrounded Therese that night and demanded that she show some respect for the house and the neighborhood, if not for us.

She agreed reluctantly. The next day, the dead rhubarb disappeared. In its place stood a small treelike thing with purple and white petunias planted around its base.

"It's a harlequin glorybower clerodendrum," Therese said excitedly when I saw the shrubby tree and shot her a skeptical look. "They smell terrific when they bloom, and they'll grow anywhere."

I just sighed. We might look alike—dark hair, blue eyes, thick black eyebrows, and as one of my boyfriends had put it, "that can opener of a nose"—but we sure didn't think alike.

I was definitely the odd person out in this picture. Therese and her gardening mania were in step with most of the city of Portland. Poke any random Portland plant, and you're likely to hit a gardener armed with pruning shears, custom-formulated potting soil, and his very own secret but surefire cures for aphids and black spot and slugs.

I admired the results these people got, and was even grateful for their dedication. Rhubarb experiments notwithstanding, it was gardeners like Therese who made walking through Portland's urban neighborhoods such a wonderful experience. But I knew I couldn't compete with them. I didn't even want to. Other stuff filled my spare time—

bike riding and running and trips to the beach and reading murder mysteries while munching on chocolate chip cookies. And Kevin.

In fact, it was because of Kevin that I became interested—but only slightly interested—in gardening. After living with my sisters for a few years, I took the plunge into the land of serious commitment. Kevin and I moved into a house together, and within days I was seized with a mysterious desire to do something cozy and domestic, something that would make a rental house a home. I ended up at the nearest nursery buying a flat of pansies, a packet of cosmos seeds, and a catnip plant for our black and white kitten, Spike. I even grabbed a small box of plant food.

As I drove home, I wondered what to do next. Did I need a gardening book? Should I pull out not-yet-recycled issues of the *Oregonian* and look for the gardening column? Maybe I should have asked someone at the nursery how to plant pansies. Or maybe, since this was the fertile Pacific Northwest, I could just throw the things in the ground, add water, and watch them grow right before my eyes, sort of like those sea monkeys advertised on the backs of comic books. After all, I just wanted a little color around the yard. I didn't want to get too involved. I certainly wouldn't be pulling weeds after dinner.

At home, I grabbed a shovel and a rusty fork-type tool left behind by a previous tenant, and headed for a neglected garden bed in the front yard. Within minutes, I fell into a rhythm remembered from all those years of forced pansy planting in Michigan: Loosen dirt. Free plant from pot. Spread roots slightly. Insert plant tenderly in ground, sprinkle on a little plant food, press soil around roots, move on. Nothing to it.

Half an hour later, as I stood there puddling water around the plants, Therese dropped by. "Those look pretty," she said. "What sort of soil amendments did you dig in?"

"What *what* did I dig in?" I asked, dripping water on my shoes.

"You know, soil amendments . . . mushroom compost, or steer manure, or bone meal, or peat moss. You *did* feed that soil before you planted flowers, didn't you?" she asked.

I shook my head, beginning to feel irritated with this bearer of bad news. I really did not want to know that I'd just spent my hard-earned dollars on plants that were going to starve to death. This is why people don't garden, I thought. It's too complicated.

"Hmmm." She looked around the yard. "That hydrangea really needs to be pruned." She walked over to a straggly rosebush and examined a few leaves. "Eeeyuck. You've got aphids here. And black spot. You'll need to spray with insecticidal soap for the aphids and strip all the spotted leaves off, or the plant will be completely ruined. And don't drop any leaves on the ground. They'll contaminate the soil and the plant will have black spot again next year."

By now, I was beyond irritated. Like the youngest member of any family, I had been receiving advice all my life. Who to date, where to go to college, what career to pursue, and which neighborhood to live in—I'd heard it all. For the most part, it was okay, even kind of touching. But every so often, one of my brothers or sisters went a little too far. Right now, Therese was going a little too far.

What made this bossy creature think she could tell me I had diseased roses? Or that my soil wasn't good enough to support plant life? I glared at her back as she contemplated the lilac tree, whose leaves,

I now noticed, were curled up like little scrolls. My fingers itched to turn the hose on her.

"Meg." She turned around just in time. "Do you have a decent gardening book?"

"Of course I don't have a gardening book," I snapped, dropping the hose back to my side and trying to look both innocent and injured. "I just want a few flowers around. I don't want a serious relationship with them!"

She regarded me silently for a moment, then started to open her mouth just as Kevin drove up with a carload of groceries "Hi, Therese. Hey, Weglet, wanna help me unload this stuff?"

"Weglet?" Therese looked at me.

I shrugged. Tracing the development of pet names is an exercise best left undone. Instead, we helped Kevin with the groceries, dropping, for the moment, the burning issues of aphids and compost and black spot and sisterly unrest.

Two days later, Therese stopped by with a well-thumbed copy of the *Western Garden Book*, an intimidatingly comprehensive gardening guide written for the masses by the high priests of Western lifestyle at *Sunset* magazine. "You can borrow this for a while," she said in an all-too-familiar well-meaning voice.

Borrow it? I didn't even want to touch it. The ten-pound, three-inch-thick tome would simply confirm what I already knew—I didn't know anything about gardening, and it was too complicated to learn without investing vast sums of time and money, neither of which I had. I just wanted to be left alone to watch my flowers succeed or fail on their own terms.

After Therese left, I stared at the book for a few minutes, then opened it and began to leaf gingerly through the pages. Ten minutes later, I closed it again. The more I read, the more depressed I got. Did I really need to know if my soil was clay or sandy, acid or alkaline? This book disapproved of me and didn't hesitate to say so: Get out there! Prune! Spray! Aerate! Divide those daylilies!

I made a cup of tea and opened the book again, deciding to concentrate on what even I knew was the most basic gardening unit: soil. After about five minutes of reading, I went outside and took a close look at the dirt that was piled up around my new flowers. It looked sort of dense and thick and slabby. It looked sort of like clay. *There*, I thought, *now I can truthfully say I got some use from that damn book*. I went back inside, picked up a murder mystery, and put all thoughts of gardening out of my head.

Western Garden spent most of the next few months lying neglected on our coffee table. Outside, the pansies bloomed. Spike the kitten swiftly annihilated her catnip plant. I bought her another. It met the same fate. The cosmos sent up feathery leaves and produced large, beautiful blooms. *Western Garden* gathered dust, and I felt vindicated.

"How's the gardening going?" Therese asked one day as autumn approached. "Is the book helping?"

I thought of the book lying alone and unappreciated in our living room. What compelling lie could I concoct? If I said yes, she'd want to have gardening conversations with me, and I'd be shown up as a fraud and an ungrateful younger sister. If I said no, I'd look like an ungrateful younger sister for keeping the book so long without using it. Either way, I lost.

"Because I kind of want it back, if that's okay," she went on.

I breathed a sigh of relief.

"But I've got another book you can have."

Oh, great, I thought. "Sure, thanks," I said.

A week later, we swapped books. This time, I was pleasantly surprised. *Introduction to Basic Gardening,* published by the same people who put out the big whompin' *Western Garden Book,* was just what it said—basic. Not too intimidating. Less than an inch thick. Barely weighed a pound. This book I could use without feeling inadequate.

During the months that followed, I picked up *Basic Gardening* every so often and leafed through it casually. For the most part, its low-key approach was exactly what I needed. I still wasn't convinced I had to know how to prune roses or divide daylilies, but I skimmed the sections about doing both. I even glanced at the section on adding soil amendments, thinking that maybe I'd take Therese's advice and feed the soil. But for something basic, it sounded awfully complex. I decided to leave my dirt to its own devices.

Any Portland resident can tell you that the Willamette River is a lot more than just a ribbon of water running through the city. It's a psychological canyon.

The Willamette divides Portland geographically and demographically. Westsiders, although they might deny it in public, often look down their noses upon those who live on Portland's eastside. The westside is best known for steep hills and steeper-priced homes. With the exception of downtown and Northwest Portland, where Therese, Elizabeth, and I lived in the mid-1980s, most westside streets are twisty, sidewalk-deprived, almost rural affairs that meander up and down and in and out of small neighborhoods and cul-de-sacs.

Eastsiders have their own brand of snobbery. "West Hills wanna-be" was a phrase I heard more than once when living on the Willamette's eastside. Eastsiders have been known to proclaim that their urban way of life is more "authentic" than that found on the city's westside. They're vocal about preferring logically laid-out city blocks and old, turn-of-the-century neighborhoods.

Some areas of Portland's eastside can give the finest westside neighborhoods a run for their money, both in terms of home sizes and prices. But take away those half-dozen neighborhoods, and what's left on the eastside can be divided into cheap construction, which will always look cheap no matter how many times new vinyl siding is put on, and block after block of charming, solid, old, tired homes awaiting the renovator's touch and the subsequent kiss of the real estate market. Grocery stores, libraries, schools, clothing boutiques, terrific restaurants, movie houses are within easy walking distance of most eastside neighborhoods. So are tattoo parlors, strip joints, hookers, adult bookstores, pool halls.

Having lived on both sides of the river, I knew where I wanted to be. I envisioned us in an old, charming home in the hills just above Northwest 23rd Avenue, now nicknamed "Trendy-third." We'd have sidewalks, a view of Mount Hood, and a house with hardwood floors and intact original architectural details. We'd be close to the action but removed from the dirt and grime of the city, which I'd had enough of during my time as an eastside resident.

Unfortunately, the homes that fit my dreams carried daunting price tags. We had two options: I could quit my freelance writing business and get a real job that would satisfy our mortgage lender's concerns about my income-producing capacity, or we could revise our house-buying plans.

Which is why I was sitting in front of a worn-down little blue house in inner Southeast Portland on a hot July afternoon. I sighed, briefly wishing I'd been born with a burning desire to be a doctor or a lawyer or a stockbroker. Then I got out of the car and walked toward the little blue house.

For the first time, I noticed a wide border of brightly colored wild-flowers that ran along the walkway to the front door. The rock garden on the steep front bank, topped with a row of healthy shrubs and a cracked, concrete birdbath, was actually sort of pretty, just as Kevin had said. In the parking strip stood two enormous maple trees, iden-tical to other maples up and down the block. It looked sort of homey. Maybe it wouldn't be so bad after all.

I checked out the homes on either side. To the west, not bad—a tidy beige and blue house with window boxes and flowers in full bloom. To the east, bad. Very bad. Sagging porch, screen door with ripped screen, light orange-colored clapboards begging for a paint job. The lawn was at least a foot high.

I sighed again and walked up the driveway. Kevin was chatting with the home's owner and introduced me to him.

"Would you like to look inside?" the owner asked politely.

"Not if you aren't prepared," I responded desperately, not quite ready to give in to economic reality.

"No, please, you're welcome to come in." He headed toward the front door and we followed.

The porch consisted of four uneven wooden steps and a concrete slab at the top. *This will not be my front porch*, I said to myself as we walked across it and through the big, beige front door that needed a paint job. The door opened directly into the living room, which was painted the most intense shade of peach I'd ever seen in captivity. I peeked into the tiny dining room, which was the same color. Beyond that was a fluorescent purple kitchen. I took in the neon striped carpet, the fifty-year-old linoleum on the countertops, and the lack of a dishwasher, oven, and garbage disposal.

Then I let my breath out in a silent sigh of relief. Thank God. No way would we move into this house.

Kevin, on the other hand, was charmed. He never even noticed the garish paint. He saw instead the hardwood floors, the ten-foot-high coved ceilings, the huge tiled fireplace, then turned around to me, his eyes sparkling. "I think this is it," he whispered.

My heart sunk. Maybe it would be out of our price range. No such luck. I prayed we'd find obvious flaws, huge flaws. We found them, all right. Kevin saw them as opportunities to get into the real estate market without breaking our budget.

Later that night, as he talked about financing options and crunched numbers on his calculator, I rattled on about how awful the house was. "That kitchen has the most disgusting carpet on the face of the earth."

"We'll install a floor," Kevin said.

"The main bedroom is painted mustard yellow," I went on.

"So we repaint," he said, continuing to punch in mysterious numbers and write down the results.

"Did you notice the house next door? It's a wreck. Location, location, location, you know." I was getting desperate.

"Umm-hmmm. But it's an up-and-coming neighborhood. Maybe those people will sell out. Or maybe they'll get shamed into fixing their house up."

"Kevin, that area's not up and coming, it's dead and gone!" I yelled, losing any semblance of control. "The house doesn't even have an oven, for God's sake! The kitchen countertops are fifty years old, the shower doesn't work, and the bathroom wallpaper is held on with straight pins and tape!"

Kevin finally looked up from his calculator. "So we get them to repair some stuff and then we write lots of checks after we move in. We're going to be there awhile. We can take things one at a time. This will be a good investment, Meg." He punched in more numbers. "Look, the way Portland is growing, any neighborhood that close to downtown is going to increase in value. The house is big enough for the two of us. It's the right price. And we've been looking for six months."

I gave up. Marriage is built on compromises, I reminded myself. This would obviously be one of them.

Chapter 2

Soil Amendments, or Getting Down and Dirty

ix weeks later, I stood in the middle of the living room in the little blue house. The bright peach room was bare except for a single floor lamp I'd just carried in from the moving truck. Mom was in the fluorescent purple kitchen, humming as she unpacked silverware and dishes. Pug and K-word, the two cats we'd adopted to fill the void left when Spike lost an argument with a car, were howling their disgust at being shut in a bedroom. Kevin was outside with a couple of brawny hired men. As I looked out at them, I noticed the vast weed population in the front yard. *Our* front yard, I reminded myself grimly. I sighed and turned my back on the early September sunlight.

Sunlight. It should have been welcome—we'd had pounding rains the week before—but within a few days, the temperature had shot back up into the eighties. I wiped sweat off my forehead just as

Therese came down the stairs that led into the living room. Like the rest of my family, she was charmed by the home's high ceilings, hardwood floors, and abundant natural light. "It's a great house, Meg. When was it built, around the turn of the century? This is a wonderful room."

"Nineteen-oh-three, and this is an orange room," I said flatly, mentally adding "Paint living room" to my to-do list, right behind "Kill weeds" and "Buy wading pool to soak feet in."

"Peach," she corrected me. "It's a nice, warm color. Did you notice you've got a Cecile Brunner in the front yard?"

"A who?"

"Cecile Brunner. That pink rosebush in the front garden bed, right near the azalea hedge, which, by the way, is going to be gorgeous in the spring. Those bushes look really healthy." She walked to the bank of divided windows that ran across the southern wall of the living room and pointed outside to a shrubby rosebush I hadn't even noticed. It was covered with tiny pink flowers. "See? It's a classic, probably planted forty years ago. You're going to love that rosebush."

I doubted that very much. I don't even like roses, much less love them. "Oh," I said. *Typical Therese*, I thought. *The turmoil of moving into a home is going on all around us, and what is she thinking of? The garden.*

Kevin came through the front door carrying a coffee table. He was followed by his father with one end of a bookcase, my father with the other end, and the two brawny men carrying our mattress. I put aside thoughts of old roses and orange walls and concentrated on directing traffic.

"Honey, come here. Did you see the cut in the bark of this tree?"

Slug Tossing

My father drew me outside and down the front-walk steps to the parking strip. "Why would anyone girdle a tree this way? They cut right through the cambium layer. Did you find out how this happened?"

"No," I admitted, looking at the deep cut that went all the way around the trunk of the biggest maple. "Think it's okay?"

He looked up at the thick green canopy of leaves overhead. "Looks like it's still alive, but I'd keep an eye on it." He walked over to the other maple and frowned. "This one has a big hole in its roots. You might get an arborist out here to look at them sometime."

"Okay, Dad." I filed it away in the back of my mind: Kill weeds, buy wading pool, paint living room, call arborist.

Later that day, when everything was off the truck, Therese and I took a moment to check the backyard. It was a vast patch of mud interrupted by weeds. "When we bought the house, this entire backyard was knee high in wildflowers," I said. "They cut them down last week after the rainstorms. I had no idea it was just dirt back here."

We walked around to the front yard, which looked better than the backyard if you didn't examine it too closely. It had grass, weeds, four wide, mostly empty flower borders, the hedge of healthy, green azaleas running across the top bank, and, of course, Cecile, the pink rosebush.

The wildflowers I'd admired in the largest border were mowed down, more victims of the recent rains. Just beneath the azalea hedge, the rock garden ran up the steep front bank. It contained several very large ferns, two or three plants with distinctive spiky branches and red berries, and a scattering of hens and chicks.

Aside from the azaleas, the two tall maples were the best thing about the home's landscaping. They looked as if they'd been planted when the house was built. A lazy cloud of bees bumbled in and out of a hole high up in the trunk of the tallest maple. Great. A beehive. I'd be plucking stingers from the cats on a weekly basis.

"Are you going to garden?" Therese asked, digging the toe of her shoe into the front garden bed.

"Yeah, a little. Nothing too serious. Just some flowers out here. And Kevin wants to do veggies in the back."

"Well, you'll want to get on it right away out here, then," Therese said. "Autumn is the best time of year to beef up the soil, and your soil needs lots of beefing. These beds look like they haven't been fed in years." She stooped down and poked her hand into the dirt. The dried-out top crust crumbled, and the soil's real nature revealed itself: dense, sticky slabs of dirt. "Clay. No surprise there. Just like most of Portland."

She straightened up, wiping her hands off on a nearby clump of grass that had strayed into the empty flower bed. "Clay is easy enough to deal with. Just dump on a bunch of steer manure, or some mushroom compost, or better yet, both, and add bone meal. Maybe peat moss, too, but be sure to wet it down first. Anything to fluff up the dirt. Add some lime, too, but keep it away from the azaleas."

"Limes? I'm supposed to put limes on my garden?"

"Not limes, *lime*. It comes powdered, in bags. It helps reduce the acidity of the soil."

"How do you know I've got acid soil?" I demanded.

"Everyone here has acid soil," she said matter-of-factly. "It's because it rains so much. The rain leaches out most of the nutrients, and what's left behind is pretty acidic."

"And why should I keep the lime away from the azaleas?" *Assuming I buy any*, I added to myself.

"Because azaleas like acidic soil. Rhodies, too. Lime sweetens the soil, raises the pH. You remember the pH scale from high school biology class, I assume." She shot me a sharp look. "Besides, your garden book should tell you all that stuff. You do still have that garden book I lent you awhile back, don't you?"

"*Introduction to Basic Gardening?*" I said. "Yeah, I have it." I didn't add that, following my complete failure at making a garden during the two years we lived in San Francisco, I had pitched *Basic* into a storage box and tried to forget about its existence. "I just don't remember anything about limes and acid."

"*Lime.* Just follow what the book says and dig in a lot of stuff, the more the better. Call me if you want to borrow the big *Sunset* book."

I suppressed a shiver. Four years had passed, and I still hadn't forgotten my demoralizing run-in with the *Sunset Western Garden Book*. It was not something I wanted to repeat. "Thanks," I said.

More than a month went by. Kevin hired someone to take care of mowing and edging our lawn. The lawn guy, Keith, was big and burly, with a long gray ponytail. He looked like he should be roaring down an interstate freeway on a Harley, terrorizing motorists and causing accidents. In reality, he had a soft voice and pleasant manner, along with plenty of knowledge about grass, plants, and trees.

"Don't you think we should mow our own lawn?" I said to my husband after Keith's first visit.

"Why? We've got too much to do to this house as it is. And we don't have a lawn mower," Kevin said.

"Maybe we could buy one next spring," I suggested.

"Sure, whatever."

I bought the wading pool and put it in the backyard. On the hottest September days, I hauled a lawn chair out of the garage, filled the pool, and soaked my feet while writing first drafts of client projects. Kevin worked long hours handling marketing and public relations for his employer, a large health care system. When the weather cooled down, I dragged my feet away from the pool, tore the sagging wallpaper off the bathroom walls, and gave the entire bathroom a fresh coat of paint. This allowed me to put off painting the living room, completely ignore the garden, and totally forget about calling an arborist.

Once or twice a week, I'd take a break and walk eight blocks south to Hawthorne Boulevard. This formerly grungy street was rapidly becoming the city's newest boutique shopping area, and I could—and did—spend hours browsing. My favorite spots for retail therapy included a cats-only shop loaded with spendy kitty toys, a bookstore named Murder by the Book, and, of course, the inescapable Starbucks coffee shop where I indulged my cafe mocha habit. Hawthorne Boulevard's pedestrians were as varied as the stores: bored, hip-looking types sporting nose rings and neon hair colors; well-dressed businesspeople congregating at restaurants; parents pushing baby strollers. "Look! Happy Americans enjoying life," Kevin said one Saturday when he accompanied me on a quest for mocha.

Hawthorne reminded me of our San Francisco neighborhood. I sat outside at Starbucks, sipping my mocha, watching the urban parade, and feeling very much at home.

In the opposite direction, two blocks north of our house, sat Laurelhurst Park. Most mornings at seven o'clock I laced on my running shoes and headed into the park's eighty acres for exercise and relatively fresh air. The park loosely marked the northern boundary of our neighborhood—Sunnyside—and the southern boundary of Laurelhurst, which is one of Portland's prettiest eastside neighborhoods.

Some days I ran through the park, across Burnside Street, and through the Laurelhurst neighborhood. But the contrast between its well-kept streets and our grimy ones was too depressing, so most days I just stayed in the park. It was a good spot for urban running. Towering trees helped screen traffic noise; flowers and shrubs made it feel like a private garden. Wooden benches were scattered along the banks of the park's lake. Ducks and birds and squirrels honked and chirped and chattered. Laurelhurst Park was a world away from the bustle and business of Hawthorne Boulevard, but it felt like home, too.

Even though I'd protested long and loud about buying into this neighborhood, I was settling in happily. Having good neighbors helped. Mary, in the house with the window boxes, was a schoolteacher raising two teenagers on her own. On the other side of us, in the broken-screen-door house, Bruce and Ed lived in seemingly long-term har-mony and commitment. Ed was a haircutter with a superb bass voice, a dedication to musical theater, and a flair for the dramatic. Bruce was quieter, but friendly. He played the flute and sold men's clothes. Connie, a cellist with the Oregon Symphony Orchestra, lived in the next house over past Bruce and Ed. On the mornings when I worked outside and Connie and Bruce practiced their instruments, the neighborhood was a very good place to be.

Among the six of us, we had two dogs and eight cats. Mary and Connie mowed their lawns and pulled weeds from their garden beds and worried about the condition of their roofs and how long they could go before having to have their houses repainted. Ed and Bruce saved their energy for more important things; Ed and Bruce threw dinner parties.

Whenever I saw Mary or Connie doing something in her yard, I'd remember with a pang of guilt that for decent flowers next spring, serious dirt work had to be done now. It wasn't the digging I feared. I was avoiding the complicated process of figuring out exactly what to dig in.

By mid-October, I ran out of excuses. A freelance writing project was wrapped up. The weather forecast promised at least two sunny days in a row. The time to dig was now, before the rains came and before more clients called.

Good soil is the foundation of a good garden, I reminded myself sternly, and remembered Therese spending endless hours digging unidentifiable muck into the front yard of the house in Northwest Portland. No wonder I'd thought gardening was such a drag. I'd be leaving for an evening bike ride with Kevin, and she'd be working off the stress of her job sweating and swearing with her plants and her dirt.

I had no illusions about producing an incredible Therese-like garden—I didn't intend to work nearly that hard—but I did want to give my plants a decent start in life. So I rounded up *Basic*, which had been languishing on the bottom of a bookshelf, paper and pencil for taking notes, and a mug of tea. October sun streamed through the living room's long bank of windows as I curled up for what I hoped would be a quick educational session. Pug, who was old and lame and almost excessively loving, climbed up onto my lap and began to purr. I scratched him behind the ears and turned to the book's very first section, "Understanding Your Soil." It was time to be enlightened.

Half an hour later, Pug was still purring and I was still unenlightened. I didn't want to think about all this stuff—salt content and nitrogen and ash and exactly how much of everything to add and what not to add. I turned the page, and encountered a spread titled "The Most Efficient Way to Dig."

Oh, great. Apparently I couldn't just get out there and hack away at the soil. No, I had to precisely angle each shovelful of dirt onto its side, so that leaves, weeds, and other junk didn't make an airtight barrier one shovel depth into the dirt. The two accompanying illustrations showed shovelsful of soil leaning neatly at an angle, and shovelsful of soil turned completely upside down, with all the debris packed tightly at the bottom. "Right," the first illustration was captioned. "Wrong," the second one thundered.

I read on. Spade, shovel, power tiller. When had *Basic* gotten so complicated?

Sullenly, I turned another page. A chart! Now, this was more like it. Here was a list of soil amendments, their pros and cons, their uses, and a few other comments, such as ash content, how well each amendment held nutrients, and if they could be used without adding nitrogen to the soil. I read for a few minutes, then began taking notes.

First, mushroom compost. According to the chart, mushroom compost could be used without adding extra nitrogen to the soil. Good. The fewer steps the better. But it was rated "poor" in the nutrient-holding category ("nutrient holding," according to the book, is a way of describing how well an amendment helps the soil retain nutrients so that plants can access them readily). Plus, it had a high ash percentage (ash, or mineral matter such as plain old dirt or gravel, is present in all amendments to some degree and makes amendments less effective). Mushroom compost didn't sound all that great, but Therese had recommended it. Who to trust, the sister or the book? I frowned, wrote "mushroom compost" on my list, and kept reading.

Dairy manure. Therese had mentioned manure, but here it was listed as a conditioner for sandy soils. As Therese had pointed out, I had the opposite—sticky, icky clay soil. But if dairy manure had worked for Therese . . . I began to write "manure" on my list, then had a sudden pungent memory of summer weeks spent with close friends at their grandparents' dairy farm. I quit writing.

Steer manure, next on the chart, was also suggested for use in sandy soils. It probably smelled bad, too. I moved on.

Peat moss. What the hell was peat moss? Therese had mentioned it, and according to the chart, it was great stuff, fluffing up the soil and rating "very good" in the nutrient-holding category. "Peat moss," I scribbled on my list.

Bark and sawdust languished at the bottom of the chart. I rejected both because they required adding nitrogen—anywhere from one-half to one pound of actual nitrogen per ten cubic feet. What was "actual nitrogen," anyway? And this cubic feet stuff—did that mean I'd have to measure how deep I dug, in addition to the length and width of the garden bed, and then do the math? Memories of physics class and convoluted mathematical calculations involving vectors and force factors made the hair on my arms stand on end. There was a reason I'd become an English major.

I stared at the list, tapping my pen on the paper. What else had Therese mentioned? Bone meal, that was it. It wasn't on the chart. I flipped to the index. Not there, either. I turned back to the beginning text on understanding soil. There it was, a single sentence that described bone meal as being loaded with phosphorus. Phosphorus? Now I had to worry about phosphorus, too? I sighed and wrote "bone meal" on my list. Maybe someone at the nursery could tell me why I needed it.

There was just one more thing to add to my shopping list—lime. It wasn't in the chart, either. The index listed something called "lime sulfur," but it was used to control plant diseases. Therese had specifically mentioned lime for correcting acidic soil. The sister won out over the reference book. "Lime," I wrote on the list.

Okay, how much of all this stuff did I need? I flipped back another page. The amendments should be at least three inches deep on the bed, maybe five. I frowned. How did that translate into how many bags to buy? I'd just have to eyeball it and hope I bought enough.

Peat moss. What the hell is peat moss? Our yard, like most yards in the Pacific Northwest, was home to a not insignificant amount of moss. (Lots of local roofs have moss, as well. Some of those roofs are so furry they bring to mind a restaurant in Door County, Wisconsin, where the roof moss is plush enough to supply food for a small herd of goats, who, chained to the roof, chew on the moss and sneer at restaurant patrons.) Couldn't I just rake moss out of the yard and use it in place of expensive bagged peat moss from the nursery?

Apparently not. Peat moss is dry and fluffy; according to an article in *American Forests* magazine that I swiped from Dad, peat moss comes from peat bogs spread across Siberia, Alaska, Canada, the Scandinavian countries, and some parts of Great Britain. It's a unique soil conditioner that's in great demand for its ability to aerate and improve a soil's nutrient-holding qualities. Basic lawn moss, which isn't even a true moss—but that's another story—is damp and ugly and essentially worthless. Lawn moss is a far cry from the soft, dark green, velvety stuff that makes such an inviting backdrop for violets and the occasional leprechaun.

In addition to being a good soil amendment, peat moss is also a nearly anonymous player in the current global-warming crisis. There are some twelve thousand million acres of peatlands stuffed with water-soaked plants decaying very, very, very slowly, all exhaling methane into the earth's atmosphere. When global warming and the increasing atmospheric load of methane are discussed, we hear about flatulent cows and we hear about the internal combustion engine. We don't hear about peatland bogs, the planet's biggest producer of methane gas. Maybe that's because peat is also the stuff that filters the water used in Scotch whiskey. In this case, the world will just have to take the bad with the good.

Fortunately for the fossil fuel supply and the global-warming crisis, the little blue house was just two minutes from a ready source of good peat moss, Portland Nursery. Our old, loud Volvo wagon, fondly dubbed "The Fleshy One" in honor of its generous proportions and beige paint job, could make the trip in ninety seconds if the traffic lights cooperated.

Portland Nursery carries plants, seeds, bulbs, shrubs, outdoor furniture, bird houses, reference books, clay pots, tools, trellises, trees— in other words, more things than I would ever need. I hummed as I parked The Fleshy One and grabbed a red wagon to haul my purchases in. First stop was the outside display of fertilizers and soil amendments.

Steer manure, chicken manure, mushroom compost, plain old compost, peat moss. It was all here. I began to drag a bag of mushroom compost off the display when I noticed signs near each pile of amendments. Curious, I stopped to read.

"The favorite way to amend soil among gardeners in the West," said the sign for steer manure. "Helps add organic matter and break up stubborn clay soils."

Clay? I could have sworn *Basic* had said steer manure was for sandy soils. Had the book been lying to me?

I read the sign near the mushroom compost bags. "Once used to grow a tabletop mushroom. Contains horse manure, chicken manure, straw, gypsum, peat moss. High pH helps balance acidic soil. *Not* for use near azaleas, camellias, other acid-loving plants."

The azalea border popped into my mind. This was getting way too complicated. I moved on.

Chicken manure didn't sound as good as steer manure, and plain old compost, I noticed, was more expensive than either. I frowned, trying to decide what to do. Just then, a nursery employee wheeled a couple of wagons back to the wagon line-up. "Excuse me," I called.

The guy came over. He had a walkie-talkie clipped on his belt. "Need some help?"

Now that I had a live source of information right in front of me, I was tongue-tied. He'd probably figure out I was clueless about amendments and walk away in disgust. "Umm, yeah, bone meal and lime?" I heard my voice slide up on the last word and cursed silently. I sounded like a wimp.

"Inside, in the room behind the cash register. Are you getting some of this stuff, too?"

"Uh-huh."

"Leave it here and have the cashier ring it up inside. That way you don't have to haul it around."

I was just getting up enough courage to ask him about steer manure versus mushroom compost when his walkie-talkie buzzed. He waved at me and walked off, talking into the instrument. At least he didn't look disgusted.

I sighed, reread the signs, and felt even more confused. This was getting me nowhere. *Okay, think about something else,* I told myself. How much should I buy of whatever I ended up with? According to the signs, each bag covered twenty-five square feet. Our biggest border, the one next to the front walk, was about three feet by fifteen feet, or forty-five square feet. I would start with two bags for that bed, and another six for the other borders.

What else was on my list? Peat moss. Huge bags of it were piled next to the mushroom compost. I hefted one. It was surprisingly light. I tossed it into the wagon and headed into the store for bone meal, deciding to put off the manure-compost decision for a few minutes.

Inside, I grabbed a medium-sized box of lime—"Corrects acid soils," read the label—and moved on to the bone meal, described as "A good source of nitrogen and phosphorus. Releases nutrients continuously. Promotes root growth. Not for acid-loving plants."

Oh, hell. Nitrogen, phosphorus, and that acid stuff again. I threw the box into the wagon anyway and wheeled over to the cashier. I'd just dump it on, try to keep it away from the azaleas, and see what happened.

"Anything else?" the cashier asked.

"Umm, yeah. Four bags each of steer manure and mushroom compost." Maybe a mixture of the two would do great things for my soil. It probably couldn't hurt.

"Do you want help loading the bags?"

"No, thanks. I can manage."

I'm pretty strong, but those bags of manure were heavier than they looked. I heaved them into the trunk, hoping I hadn't strained any important muscles, then drove home, heaved them out again, and took a lunch break.

While I chewed a tuna sandwich and tried to ignore the cats purring and winding around my legs, I called Kevin.

"I've got a whole load of soil amendments I'm digging into those front borders today and tomorrow." And you'd better appreciate it, my tone of voice said. The cats progressed from purring to yowling, and I dropped two chunks of tuna on the floor.

"That's great. Thanks so much for doing it." The gratitude was obvious in his voice, and I knew it wasn't just because he was putting in such long hours at work.

"Yeah, I know. Your mother was a slave driver."

"She was! Every Saturday morning, she'd have me out there weeding and edging and sweating in the sun. Never again. There's no future in hard work."

"Right." We'd had this conversation before. Poor Kevin, forced into providing cheap labor for his gardening-obsessed mother. Hey, I'd been there. I'd done it, too—pansies, lettuce, tomatoes—protesting the whole time. Yet here I was, for some strange reason volunteering—volunteering!—to work in the garden. Perhaps I was more like my mother and my sisters than I wanted to admit. I dropped more tuna on the floor for the cats. Another cup of tea, and then I'd get to work.

Common sense dictates that dumping huge bags of dirt food on top of a bunch of weeds will produce not only better soil, but a population explosion of even better weeds. I spent that entire afternoon yanking weeds from the four flower borders.

My weeding technique was rudimentary, at best. I gathered a receptacle—in this case, the lid of the garbage can—and our old, rusty hand fork. Then I got down on my hands and knees and pulled up every green thing in sight. I also unearthed bits of glass, rusted beer-bottle caps, nails, and old cigarette butts.

As the garbage can lid filled up, I'd walk back to the garage, empty the lid into the garbage can, and take a minute to stretch. By the time the borders were relatively weedless, rain was dribbling down.

Rain dribbles down a lot in Portland. Sunny skies give way to showers with little warning and for no apparent reason. Years ago, in the middle of August, Therese was married in a Portland park. It poured the entire weekend; the tents they'd rented to provide shade from the expected sunshine sagged under the weight of the rainwater. The mercury never got above 55 degrees. That marriage didn't last, but the memories of the wedding sure did. Nine years later, Kevin and I were married in August. It was 102 degrees. Neither the church nor the reception hall had air conditioning. Guests and groomsmen alike teetered—literally—on the edge of passing out. I'm not sure which wedding was a more miserable weather experience.

Now, I glared at the sky as the dribbles turned to bona fide raindrops. Bruce came walking up the street, sensibly sheltered under a large black umbrella.

"Why are you out here working in the rain?" he asked. *Typical yuppie homeowner*, his voice said.

"I'm not. I'm just heading inside." I stood up.

"You're going to make our yard look bad, aren't you? I suppose you'll be out here all the time pulling weeds and pruning your roses." By now Bruce was on his porch, shaking his umbrella dry.

"Hardly. I'm not a gardener, hey? And I don't even like roses."

"'Hey?'" Bruce echoed my unconscious speech mannerism. "You

didn't grow up here, did you? Where, Wisconsin?"

"Michigan." My cheeks were hot. I tried a smile. "Still shows, huh?"

"Oh, girl." Bruce shook his head, smiling. He pulled open the ripped screen door, unlocked the front door, and went inside. His dog, Hoffmann, immediately let loose a chorus of loud, joyful barks, and Bruce and Ed's two cats ran out onto the porch.

I gathered up my tools and headed inside. The rain stopped twenty minutes later, but by then I was in a steaming hot tub, soaking my sore muscles and reading a murder mystery.

Around noon the next day I grabbed our shovel, which we'd found in the garage when we moved in, and got ready for some intense digging. I slit open a bag of steer manure and took a cautious sniff. Not too bad. Then I tried to lift the bag and pour the contents right on the garden bed. But after lying in a wet garden bed all night, the manure had soaked up moisture and was too heavy to lift. A quick search of the garage yielded a dented metal bucket, with which I emptied the bag until I could pick it up and coax out the remaining manure. A bag of mushroom compost, dumped on the half of the bed farthest from the azaleas, followed the steer manure. Then I opened the bag of peat moss, pulled some out, squirted it lightly with the hose, and spread it on top of the compost. Bone meal and lime came next; I kept the lime away from the azaleas. The resulting pile was nearly six inches thick.

I was ready to dig.

Slug Tossing

I love dirt, especially in the form of mud. As a kid, squishing a big handful of mud between my fingers was the ultimate combination of visual and tactile experiences. I made mud pies, and decorated them with twigs and leaves and rocks and the occasional dead bug. I threw mud at other children, smeared mud on my sunbaked legs and arms. Little did I know that in exclusive spas all over the world, people were paying outrageous sums of money to be pampered in mud baths. I just knew it felt good.

Today, the ground was still a bit damp from yesterday's short rain, but not too muddy to dig. I worked, chopping the soil into small chunks, not worrying about angling it precisely on its side as *Basic* dictated. The sun shone. At one point, I stepped backward into a small mud puddle. It squooshed. And with that sound, I was suddenly reliving my all-time-great mud experience.

I was about ten when, either out of boredom or creativity, my brother Mark decided to flood part of our large backyard. The entire neighborhood played ball there, and over the years the grass between home plate and the pitcher's mound had almost entirely surrendered its will to live. Mark turned the hose on the exposed dirt, and within minutes we had a wide river of mud.

We also had a crowd of kids eager to play in it. Mark was thirteen, the oldest of the neighborhood crowd and a born leader. He quickly grasped the potential for chaos and imposed some basic rules: Stand in line if you want to slide. No pushing, no cuts. No throwing mud balls at the person sliding. Typical kid rules, governing typical kid behavior.

But not even Mark could enforce discipline forever. Within less than thirty minutes, anarchy broke out. Collisions took place. Fights erupted. By the time Mom looked out the kitchen window, we had degenerated to packing mud into our socks and beating on each other. I took a mud ball in the ear and returned fire. Two, maybe three little kids were crying; at least one was trampled underfoot. My braids were solid dirt. I have never been so filthy in my entire life, and it was glorious.

Now, twenty years older and supposedly somewhat wiser, I barely noticed the strain in my shoulder and back muscles as the shovel plunked through layers of peat moss and bone meal and lime and compost and steer manure down into the heavy soil. But when I reached the end of the final garden bed, nostalgia had worn off. I was just plain sore. The pain across my shoulders, the blisters stinging my bare hands were painfully obvious. After hours of digging, with one short stop for tea and cookies, it was time to throw in the shovel for the day.

I poked the soil in a few random places. The big, heavy, clay chunks were broken up into significantly smaller chunks. It would take several years of hard work to turn this stuff into nice, crumbly dirt—"loam," as *Basic* called it—but at least I'd made a start.

I trudged slowly back to the garage, toting the shovel and wishing I had both an on-call masseuse and a rototiller.

Then I headed inside for a long, hot soak in the tub. I needed it even more than I had twenty years earlier.

Chapter 3

I Say Seed, You Say Sod, Let's Call the Whole Thing Off

aagh! Kitty, c'mere!" I chased Pug through the house, trying to grab him before his muddy paws could inflict more dirt on my just cleaned hardwood floors. For an old, arthritic, lame-in-one-leg cat, he could really move when he wanted. Apparently, the sight of me with a towel and a crazed expression on my face was enough to put those kitty legs in motion.

By the time I caught him, most of the mud had been deposited throughout the downstairs. I wiped his paws off anyway, threw the towel down the laundry chute, released the struggling cat, and hollered up the stairs, "Kev? We have to do something about all this mud!"

"What?" Kevin hollered back.

I marched up the stairs. Our bedroom was downstairs, as was my office, and Kevin had claimed the second floor as his own. Now, he was sitting at his desk, his dark blond head bent over some project he'd brought home from work.

I looked around the second floor and sighed. This area, like the rest of the house, was in serious need of attention. It was divided into two spaces: a small room under the front dormer, and the room we were now in, a long, large area that ran the width of the house and had small windows at either end. The walls slanted in at steep, seemingly random angles and met overhead in a low ceiling. They had apparently been painted at different times by different people, and ranged from beige to peach to deep green to plain old primer white. A cheap, extremely maroon carpet covered the floor.

I flopped down on the carpet near Kevin's desk. "Good Lord, where do you suppose they found this stuff?" I asked, rolling a strand between my fingers. "It feels like a bad-quality polyester sweater."

"Probably got it as a remnant," Kevin said, stretching and cracking his neck.

I winced. "Don't *do* that."

"Sorry." He smiled. "What were you hollering about?"

"Mud. Pug just tracked mud from the backyard through the entire downstairs. Do you remember how Spike used to come in from the rain and go to the drawer where the rags were kept and then stand there until someone dried her off? Pug hates being dried off."

"I still can't believe we didn't notice there was no grass under all those wildflowers," Kevin said.

"Yeah." I had a clear mental picture of the former owners preparing to put the house on the market. In my mind, they were crouched over a book titled *How to Sell Your Home FAST*. Tip #3 in the lawn and garden section undoubtedly read, "Unsightly backyard? Don't panic! Sprinkle wildflower seed, water well, and wait for the buyers to pound at your door."

"I guess we really should put some grass in," Kevin said. "The last time Keith was here doing the lawn I asked him about putting in grass. He said we could do it this time of year."

I frowned. "Put in grass in late October? Hang on." I ran downstairs and came back up with *Basic*. "Some stuff in here about how to do it. Nothing about when to do it," I reported. "Hey, as long as we're buying grass seed, there's a big spot on the west end of the front yard that needs help, too. It's all weeds and bare dirt right now."

Kevin was giving me an odd look. Obviously I'd lost him somewhere. "Grass seed?" he asked. "You think we should buy grass seed?"

"You got a better way to grow a lawn?"

"Yeah. Hire someone to put down sod."

"Hire someone? Sod? Why would we do that?"

"Why not?" he countered. "I'm not going to do all that work. First you have to pull all the weeds, then rent a bunch of machines and dig up the soil and add fertilizer and stuff, then put the seed on, then keep it wet for weeks to make sure it sprouts. I remember my dad doing it when we moved into our new house. I'm not spending my weekends that way."

"Oh, come on, it can't be that complicated," I argued.

He shook his head. "Why on earth would you want to do it? It's so much work."

"I dunno. It just seems like the sort of thing homeowners do. You know, hang curtains, mow the lawn, plant grass. Plus sod seems like—

well, kind of like buying a prefab home. We might as well put in Astroturf."

We argued on and off for the rest of the evening. Kevin wouldn't budge. He was not going to dig up our yard and plant grass seed, and that was all there was to it.

"So, okay," I said finally, "how are you going to do this? Just hire somebody we don't even know and turn them loose on our lawn?"

"There's a whole section in the paper where landscapers advertise. They all have business licenses, Meg. It's not like they're out there ripping off the public every day."

"No, just the day they work for us."

The battle continued. Kevin wanted an instant lawn, and, beyond writing a check, refused to lift a finger to get one. I remained convinced that we'd appreciate the grass more if we did it the old-fashioned way. I wanted to see green shoots of grass coming up and know I'd made it happen. Besides, it couldn't really be as much hard work as he insisted.

Eventually, we reached a compromise. Kevin would have sod installed in the backyard; I would take care of seeding the big bare spot in the front yard.

Once we'd agreed to go our separate ways in the yard, Kevin set up appointments with four small landscaping firms. "I asked these guys about our timing," he reported. "They all said it's perfect. This is the best time to lay sod."

"Of course they're going to say that," I said. "This is probably their slow time." As much as I wanted to cover up the mud in our backyard, it seemed logical that roots would take hold and grass would sprout more easily in warm weather than in cool.

Kevin gave me that look that said he was just about to lose patience. "Meg, why are you so argumentative? Trust me on this; they're all really busy right now. I had trouble setting times up with these guys, they're so swamped. This is prime time to transplant trees and shrubs and put in lawns. If you do it now, the sod has time to reestablish its roots before the really cold weather hits, then it just sort of hunkers down all winter long. If you do it in the spring, it has to put its roots down and start growing all at the same time."

"Oh," I said, my warm-weather root-growing theory shot to pieces.

"It's the same thing with trees and shrubs," he went on. "Plant them now, and the roots have time to reestablish their root systems. Plus, if you transplant something when it's dormant, it's less of a shock. The plant has a better chance of surviving and being healthy."

Leave it to Kevin to thoroughly investigate anything he's going to get involved with, I thought. It was just one of the many differences between us. I jump into things feet first, convinced I'll figure out how to do something after I've said I'll do it ("Okay, I'll seed the yard myself . . . "). Kevin prefers to test the water before committing himself. And test. And retest. How many years had we dated before he popped the question? That should have been my first clue.

The landscaping guys showed up the next weekend at precisely staggered time intervals. Kevin took each one around the backyard, describing what he wanted done. I just hung around, radiating silent disapproval.

"I think I'd like about a yard left bare on those three sides," he told the first landscaper, "and about six feet on this side, where the fruit trees will go."

Fruit trees? This was the first I'd heard about fruit trees.

"And what's going into the borders?" the guy asked.

"Strawberries along the fences and vegetables against the garage," came the reply.

That was the first I'd heard of that, too. I knew he'd wanted to plant a few vegetables, but not two whole borders' worth.

"I thought you didn't want anything to do with the yard," I said accusingly, after the landscaper had left.

"Not the yard, no. *Growing* things is different. It'll be fun."

I just shook my head. I should have known that a guy born and raised in Portland would have some genetically predetermined interest in gardening, even if years of edging the lawn and pulling weeds for his parents had nearly wiped it out.

The parade of landscapers continued. They all had two things in common. First, they insisted on massive chemical intervention to get rid of the weeds. "A good strong contact herbicide's the only thing that'll get those weeds out," one of them said. "We'll spray each weed, then come back in a week when they're dead, pull them out, and start putting the lawn in."

"Can't you just pull the weeds by hand?" I asked, drawn into the conversation in spite of myself.

The man looked at me as if I'd just arrived from another planet. "Takes too long. Costs too much. Doesn't work as well as herbicide."

"I don't want poison in my yard," I said stubbornly. "We have cats. They'll pick it up on their paws and lick it off. It's not good for the environment, either."

The guy refrained from rolling his eyes, but I could tell it was a struggle. "We can keep the cats inside after the yard is sprayed, until the sod gets put down," Kevin said. I glared at him. He ignored me.

The second thing they all agreed on was our front yard. It was a mess, and we should have sod laid there as well.

"Couldn't help but notice what bad shape this front lawn is in. See this stuff?" one of the guys said, pointing to what looked like a carpet of dead grass clippings near the roots of the grass. "That's thatch. It's basically matted, dead grass. You need to get rid of it. And this should all be aerated, too. We use a machine that drills holes into the lawn. Getting up the thatch and aerating the lawn helps the ground breathe. Makes the grass grow better. And we'll take care of those big weeds, too. Little squirt of herbicide will take them right out."

I didn't bother to explain that I wanted to look out the window one morning and see, glowing against the black dirt, that impossibly bright green color of brand-new grass, and know that I'd done it all myself, and that the environment wasn't any worse off because of it. Men who relied on herbicides, noisy machines, and a Mat-O-Grass simply wouldn't understand.

We walked around to the foot of the driveway and stood in the street watching the landscaper drive off. "When's the next guy due?" I asked.

Kevin checked his watch. "Five minutes."

"And what home improvement project are you embarking on now?" Bruce, accompanied by his collie, Hoffmann, came out of the house and joined us in the street.

"Sod for the backyard," Kevin said.

Bruce twitched an eyebrow. "It's been mud back there ever since we've been here, and we've been here for nine years. I guess they did most of their work inside the house."

I snorted. Kevin laughed. Bruce's eyebrow went back up.

"Fresh paint, yeah, but the colors!" As I began to describe the choice of paint colors in the house, a large guy on a bicycle came pedaling down the street. When he saw Bruce he started yelling. "Fag" was the only printable thing that came out of his mouth; when he got near us he ran his bike right at Bruce, narrowly missing him. The three of us instinctively backed out of the street and onto the driveway.

That's when I started screaming back. "Shut up, you jerk! Get out of here!" My voice slid up an octave, and I shrieked like a magpie.

The guy circled his bike around, shouting angrily at me. I backed up a little farther. Then he sped off down the street and around the corner.

"Who was that?" Kevin said, putting his arm around me and drawing me close. I was trembling and near tears.

"Welcome to the neighborhood," Bruce said. His normally pale cheeks were flushed a startling red. "That's one of our favorite knuckle-draggers. There's about six of them, all brothers. They live right around the corner in that big rundown white house."

"You put up with this?" I asked angrily, tears now rolling down my face. I wiped my nose with the back of my hand. "Can't you call the cops or something?"

Bruce shrugged. "We have. We can file a complaint, but unless we're actually attacked, there's not much the cops can do."

"Isn't there some sort of antiharassment ordinance or something?"

Bruce shrugged again. "It doesn't happen that often. You live with it. C'mon, Hoffmann." He waved at us, and they walked off down the block.

I stared at Bruce's back. I was still trembling. "That does it. We're moving to the suburbs."

Kevin was silent for a moment. "Sure, if you want. But there are jerks in the suburbs, too. You want me to call the cops? Are you okay?"

I sighed. "I'm fine. I just can't believe we live in a neighborhood where this sort of stuff goes on." I slid my arm around his waist. We stood silently until the next landscaper drove up.

The following Monday, I drove out to one of Portland's westside industrial parks to deliver the final draft of a marketing brochure to a client. The lawns in front of my client's building and all the nearby offices were an almost shocking shade of green. I walked over to the grass and took a close look: no dandelions, no clover, no weeds of any type. Just a thick carpet of green blades. It was positively unnatural. How many pounds of chemicals were needed to achieve this weed-free nirvana?

As I drove back toward the freeway, I spotted a likely reason for the lush grass: the offices of a commercial lawn-care service just three doors down from my client. I yanked hard on The Fleshy One's steering wheel and within a few minutes was in the building's lobby, perusing an informational brochure and smiling at the receptionist.

"Hi." I smiled, trying to hide my true intent. "Could someone tell me about your lawn-care services?"

"Sure." The woman punched a button. "Gayleen? Can you come out here for a minute?" She smiled at me. "Gayleen will be right out."

Gayleen was enormously pleasant and informative. Yes, their firm did all the fertilizing and weed control for the industrial park. Did I work for a company that needed lawn-care services? No? Well, was I interested in their residential lawn-care program? They provided fertilization every five weeks, with herbicidal sprays on clover and any broadleaf weed, such as dandelions. (*Clover? They'd have to spray my entire lawn.*) They applied lime once a year and eradicated lawn moss in the early spring. And they would aerate the lawn as well. "But you have to be sure you're watering regularly when the lawn is aerated," Gayleen said.

"What do you use on the weeds?" I asked.

"It's just a hormone spray," she said earnestly. "It's completely natural. It cuts off the food supply from the root of the plant to the top, so the weed starves to death. Hormones aren't bad for the environment. And our fertilizers contain nitrogen, potassium, and phosphorus, which are found in all living things. So they're totally natural, too."

"But what's in it?" I asked. "The weed spray, I mean. What's the name of the hormone?"

Gayleen's smile slipped a little. "It's just a hormone. Really, it's totally natural."

I thanked her and left, feeling like I'd just watched a Dow Chemical commercial.

Do I even want a lawn? I asked myself as I drove home. Maybe it would be more ecologically sensitive to just let the lawn live or die on its own terms. Gayleen might say they used only hormones and naturally occurring compounds, but I was willing to bet all that stuff would have a detrimental effect on the environment. And as for having a regular watering schedule, it would be hard enough to keep up with the flowers, much less to remember to sprinkle the lawn. Besides, this was Portland, land of the waterlogged. Why on earth would I be watering the lawn? It seemed like a stunningly stupid use of a resource, not to mention that it would send money directly out of our checking account and into the Water Bureau's coffers.

Maybe I needed to rethink this lawn thing. Maybe I needed some expert advice from a disinterested party. Maybe . . .

When I got home, I grabbed the phonebook, looked up the number for Portland Nursery, and dialed. I'd seen people at the nursery's information desk, juggling phones in one hand and huge reference books in the other. I explained my predicament to the person who answered the phone and was put through to the lawn-care expert.

"That's 2,4-D they're using on the weeds," said the voice on the other end of the line. "Technically, yeah, it's a hormone. It's also a known carcinogen in dogs. It's similar to the Agent Orange stuff that was used in the Vietnam War."

"Oh," I said.

"2,4-D does photodegrade, but the problem—and this has been documented—is that it gets tracked inside on shoes or clothes, and then it gets into carpets, where it takes a very, very long time to break down."

"We've got three cats," I said. "I don't think I want them playing in this stuff."

"You don't. I don't have kids yet, but I plan to, and no kid of mine is going to play on a treated lawn. Besides, there's a whole other issue here. One of my neighbors uses a lawn service, and I can always tell when the service has been there because there will be fertilizer pellets all over the sidewalk. That stuff gets washed into the storm drains, and it makes the water too nitrogen-rich, and contributes to algae bloom, and it's just a real mess."

"So what's my option? Let the lawn just do whatever it wants?"

He laughed. "You could. Or we've got a totally organic fertilizer here that you could use. It's more expensive, but you don't have to use it as often. Some of our customers apply it just once a year, in the fall. You might want to use it in spring, early summer, and fall for the first year or two."

"Just three times? Not every five weeks?"

"No. Three times should do it, and then cut back to once a year. See, the organic compounds stay on the lawn better; they don't wash away, and after a few years of use, they actually build up a nutrient reserve in the soil. A study done at Oregon State proved that. Nothing like that's been shown with the nonorganic fertilizers."

"Maybe I should just bag the whole idea of a lawn," I mused.

"Lots of people are letting their lawns go natural, or growing vegetables in their front yards," he said. "Sometimes neighbors aren't real thrilled about that. But an awful lot of water and chemicals and money can be sunk into keeping a lawn green. You'll have to decide if that's what you really want."

Well, did I really want a lawn? Two days later I was still pondering that question. I knew I didn't want to grow vegetables in the front yard—a few flowers would be about all I could handle—but maybe I should just let the lawn go its own way.

But, I reasoned, it was just a tiny patch of grass that I was seeding. It's not as if it would take a huge amount of water to keep the seedlings wet, or an enormous amount of time to watch over them. And the reward would be fresh, green grass, clean and sweet enough to nibble on.

Decision made, I hauled out the gardening book and opened it to the section on planting lawns. It was just two pages long, one full page of which was illustrations. *This shouldn't be too awful.* I settled down to read and take notes.

It was worse than awful. In fact, it looked like an absolutely hellish project. "Nine Steps to a New Lawn" called for doing far more work with far more lawn machines than I had ever dreamed existed. After the first discouraging readthrough, I sighed, re-read the nine steps, and glumly studied the accompanying illustrations. Maybe Brawny Man's Mat-O-Grass wasn't such a bad idea, after all.

Then I read the instructions a third time and perked up a bit. There were a few places where I could cut corners. I could even skip an entire step or two. It didn't have to be a textbook example of a new lawn. It just needed to be better than what was there—no hard feat.

The first step called for completely removing the existing grass with a power sod cutter, whatever that was. Okay, I could deal with this. There *was* no existing grass, just weeds and dirt. All I had to do was put in some time pulling weeds. I'd done that before.

I'd done step two before, as well: Pile on vast quantities of soil amendments.

Step three, however, lost me completely. It involved a rotary tiller, which looked like one of those huge, heavy floor polishers I'd once used to buff our wood floors—only more dangerous. This thing had large, sharp, exposed blades on the bottom so that it could effectively slice the soil and anything else that got in its way. I had a sudden vision of what would happen if the rotary tiller escaped from me the way the floor polisher had. Maybe blood is a good soil amendment. Maybe I'd better dig up my sturdy old hiking boots and wear them if I used this machine.

It wasn't just the equipment that looked scary. The instructions did, too. They called for tilling the soil six to nine inches deep, crossing over my own tracks several times. Only in this way would the dirt and the amendments applied in step two be thoroughly, properly mixed, the book warned.

At this point, I put the book down. Temptation loomed. Once again, I'd led with my mouth, and now I was in trouble. Was it too late to call the landscaper? Maybe he'd even thatch and aerate the grass.

Then I rallied. *I am woman, hear me roar.* It was time to get creative. There was a shovel in our garage, wasn't there? Shovels could be used to dig dirt, couldn't they? I could do this; all I needed was a little encouragement.

I picked up the phone and called Therese.

"You ever put in a lawn?"

"Good God, no. Don't tell me you're doing that backyard by yourself?"

Great. Even my gardening-obsessed sister was on my husband's side. "No," I replied. "I'm just adding some seed to the bare spots on the front lawn."

"Oh, that shouldn't be too hard. Just dig in a bunch of amendments and sow the seed. Get all the weeds out first. Just like planting flowers." She sounded a little too breezy.

"You ever done this?" I repeated.

"No, but it should work. Want to borrow any gardening books?"

That got me off the phone in a hurry.

The next three steps were easier to deal with. I wasn't going to install permanent sprinklers, so I could skip step four entirely. Step five said to drag the surface of the soil with a board scraper, which looked like a large board attached to a long, T-shaped handle. This would level the dirt. I decided to use the flat back of our rusty metal rake instead. Step six called for firming the soil with a roller. The drumlike implement shown looked less evil than the rotary tiller, but still capable of efficiently mashing a foot or two. I would definitely skip step six. Maybe I'd walk around on the dirt a bit to pack it down.

On to the final three steps. These I could handle. Sow the seed. Rake the surface to even it out. Put on a light layer of mulch and water well. End of project.

Piece of cake, I thought. All I needed now was grass seed, a few more bags of amendments, and several hours of spare time.

Is it wise to buy grass seed at the same store where you purchase groceries and personal hygiene products? I stood in the garden center at Fred Meyer and pondered this burning question. On the one hand, it was, well, handy. On the other hand, as is so often the case at Fred Meyer, there were just too damn many items from which to choose.

Brands and types of grass seed in brightly colored boxes crowded the shelves. Large sweeps of improbably green lawn and promises of resilient, weed-free turf shrieked from the front of each box. How could I ever decide which one was right for my little piece of lawn? I headed grass seedless to the checkout stand, deciding to go somewhere that felt friendlier and less overwhelming.

When I pulled The Fleshy One into Portland Nursery's parking lot later that day, the little red wagons were lined up and waiting. I grabbed one and wheeled it through the outdoor display of plants— pansies, dusty miller, ornamental kale. The pansies looked sweet and tender but, along with the other plants, were tough enough to make it through all but the harshest winter weather. Looking at them reminded me of how bare the front border was. Having some plants in that border would cut down on the kitty-mud factor, wouldn't it? By the time I made it inside to the grass seed, the wagon was crammed with flowers.

The grass-seed display at Portland Nursery was small and easy to handle. There were two different brands of seed—Portland Nursery's house blend and a regional supplier's—and two different types within each brand, for sunny areas or shady areas.

Our front lawn was mostly sunny, with partial shade in the afternoon from the tall maples on the parking strip. I flipped the Portland Nursery Sun Lawn Seed bag over. "Tolerates moderate shade," it said. This, then, was the grass seed for me. It was made up of perennial ryegrasses, Seville and Dandy, and mixed with Aurora hard fescue. Who would take the time to name grass? I wondered, and, just out of curiosity, looked at the bag formulated for shady areas. The grass names on this one were even better: Cindy red fescue, Elka perennial ryegrass, and Enjoy Chewings fescue. Too bad the lawn wasn't shady. "Yes, that's my Enjoy Chewings out there," I could say, waving nonchalantly at the yard. "Along with Cindy and Elka, of course."

Strategically placed right next to the seed were boxes of new-lawn starter, which is basically fertilizer fine-tuned for lawns as opposed to vegetables or flowers. The numerals 10-30-30 were printed in large type on the front of each box. On the back, the numbers were explained as the percentages of nitrogen, phosphorus, and potassium. Phosphorus, the label said, promotes root growth. As I read, I remembered that phosphorus was one of the elements in bone meal. And phosphorus was on the periodic table of the elements that I'd studied back in junior high and high school, wasn't it? I'd dug phosphorus into my flower borders just a short time before. Phosphorus and I went way back. I wedged a small box of lawn starter (organic) into the wagon, next to the flowers and the grass seed.

"Anything else?" the clerk asked as she rang up my purchases.

"Yeah, two bags each of steer manure and mushroom compost." This time, I didn't think twice about which to buy. It was too early to tell if this combination was doing great things in the borders, but at least I was familiar with it.

At home, I dragged the big bags from the trunk of the car and left them lying on the driveway. Then I gathered my weed-eradicating equipment—the rusty hand fork, the top of the garbage can lid—and went at it.

It's amazing how Zen-like weed pulling can be. Loosen weed from soil, shake off excess dirt, toss weed into receptacle, move on to next weed. We had enough weeds to keep me in a meditative state for hours.

After a short time, both cats appeared and sniffed at the garbage can lid, where I was piling weed carcasses. Pug curled up for a nap under Cecile, who was still sprouting tiny, perfectly formed pink roses. K-word crouched at the base of the wooden fence that separated our yard from Mary's. A squirrel in Mary's hawthorne tree chattered loudly, daring K-word to come up and duke it out. She growled. Birds chirped. The sun shone.

It was positively pastoral.

I pulled and pondered. Some weeds are actually quite pleasing to the eye: fluffy white clover, cheerful yellow dandelions. But they were growing where I didn't want them to be—the age-old definition of a weed—so I yanked them out, along with the rest of the plants that had moved into this patch of dirt. One resident had purply little flowers, and another one looked awfully familiar—was it bindweed? I'd heard Therese and Elizabeth shrieking about bindweed when we lived together in Northwest Portland. According to them, it had a fondness for flower borders and vegetable beds. I now had proof that it loved plain old lawns as well.

The bindweed was actually sort of pretty, with tiny white flowers. But those delicate flowers masked the bindweed's ruthless nature. Each hunk of above-ground weed was attached to tough, teeny roots that spiked off in all directions and only reluctantly gave up their grasp on the dirt. Soon, instead of sticking to my original plan of methodically, meditatively weeding each square foot of lawn, I was scrambling around the yard like a large, particularly ungainly crab, swearing and sweating, pulling up feathery lengths of weed and root and following wherever the strands led, all the while dragging the garbage can lid behind me. My Zen-like state was pretty well shot.

Finally, I gave up on the bindweed. The dozen or so remaining weeds—wide, flat, tough, broadleafed, and ugly—destroyed my few remaining shreds of composure. These dinner plate–sized weeds were vicious, and the first one I attacked won the battle handily. I hacked at it with my hand fork, trying to get the main root loose. The top four inches of root came out, but the rest of it remained in the ground, ready to send up a brand-new, perfectly healthy weed. I hacked some more and succeeded in putting a dent in my left forefinger. Damn! No wonder so many people used herbicides.

It was time to call out my own version of heavy artillery—our secondhand shovel. I dug the blade deep into the ground around the weed's tap root and wedged most of it out, along with a huge amount of dirt, which left a gaping hole in the yard. I shook off as much dirt as I could, but a definite hole remained. Then, shovel poised for destruction, I moved on to the next weed. Soon my tiny piece of ground was full of miniature craters. It wasn't pretty. It wasn't easy. But it was working.

So was I. We were having a mild heat wave, the type that sometimes comes to Portland in October. The temperature was probably somewhere in the mid-seventies. Perspiration poured off my forehead, my forearms, my chin, and the back of my neck. "You could have hired some hefty guy to do all this work, but noooo," a voice said in my head. "You had to do it yourself."

"It'll be worth it," I said out loud, stubbornly. No nasty-looking weed, no matter how tough, could keep me from having self-planted, chemical-free, freshly sprouted grass.

When I was growing up, the neighborhood kids congregated in our huge backyard for endless games of baseball. Our lot was both deep and wide, about a quarter of an acre smack in the middle of a small-town city block. The backyard was big enough to hold a baseball diamond (small), a six-hole golf course (ditto), long hedges of lilacs, a sandbox and a swing set, two huge black walnut trees (one complete with tree house), and a patio. When we felt the urge to play croquet or badminton or volleyball, we hauled the equipment into the backyard. It was kid paradise.

As a child, of course, I'd taken all that wonderful open green space for granted, the same way I'd accepted our huge brick home with the third-floor ballroom and indoor basketball court. Now, as I pulled weeds and dripped sweat, the thought of having that much grass to care for was overwhelming. I could barely cope with a small section of a small urban plot. What would I have done with an enormous lawn? Not to mention the fact that vast expanses of lawn are currently looked down upon as being somewhat indulgent and decadent. All that grass where you could be growing vegetables . . . All that water used to keep all that grass green, when the water could be diverted to better uses like spilling baby salmon over the dams in the Columbia River . . . All that precious wasted space, when everyone knows that density is the name of the game in today's urban environment.

I dug out the last of the huge broadleaf weeds and headed indoors for a long, hot bath, undoubtedly another watery indulgence. Some days it's hard to know which vices are okay and which are on the culture police hit list.

The next day dawned cold and clear. This day's work would be easy: No weeds to pull. No need to crawl around on my knees. Just plain old digging, followed by the fun of actually sowing grass seed.

Using the shovel instead of the *Basic*-recommended tiller, I dug in the amendments as deeply as I could. Then, with the old metal rake turned prong side up, I tried to smooth out the hills and valleys in the dirt. After several passes, the dirt looked fairly level—not perfect by any means, but good enough. Then I walked across the dirt several times, trying to tamp it down without leaving deep footprints. The result wasn't perfect, but it would do.

I'd planted seeds before, always flowers. This was different. Instead of digging holes and putting individual seeds inside, I would be broadcasting the tiny grass seed across the top of the dirt. *Basic* showed a mechanical seed spreader that looked like a lawn mower with a box on top. We didn't have one of those stashed in the garage, so I opted for the time-honored method of handcasting, which is what farmers and peasants did for all those centuries before agricultural machines came along.

Ideally, handcasting involves marching slowly across the lawn, sweeping your arm from side to side in front of you, all the while letting the grass seed fall in an even spray on the ground. Here's what really happened: I got the march down right away. Even the arm waving was easy to master. But the seed came out from between my fingers in big spurts and miserly dribbles. At the end of my first march over the lawn, I turned around and saw patches of bare dirt surrounded by little areas mounded with seed. The second march produced marginally better results, the third and fourth a little better than the second. Obviously, there was a skill needed for this, and it took more than ten minutes to learn it.

Some grass seed still clung to my hands when I was done. I dusted it off above one of the bare patches. Then I picked up seed from the thickest clumps and sprinkled it over the remaining bare dirt. Finally, I took the old metal rake, turned it prong side down, and gently raked through the seed in an attempt to further even out the distribution.

Next, I gathered a ball of twine, a pair of scissors, and four wooden stakes I'd found in the garage, one of which looked suspiciously like an old toilet plunger handle. The main object of staking off the newly seeded area was to keep the cats off the dirt while the seed germinated. I pushed the stakes into the ground, then ran twine from stake to stake at three different levels, hoping it would be an effective kitty deterrent. Then, using the spray nozzle on the garden hose, I watered my new lawn just enough to lightly wet the entire area without soaking it.

By now, my stomach was reminding me that lunch was long overdue, but I wanted to plant the winter flowers before packing up for the day. I placed the plants in little groups throughout the front garden bed and stood back to study the effect. It didn't look right. Somehow, what had been a lush crowd of color and texture at the nursery was at home pools of dirt interrupted by stiff-looking flowers. The bed could have held three times as many plants and not been overpopulated. Feeling a little depressed, I rearranged the plants a few times, then gave up and planted them where they stood. The finished product was fluffy and colorful in some parts, bare in others—sort of like a long-haired calico cat with a bad case of mange.

Later, as I scrubbed the last of the dirt from my hands and thought about what to make for lunch, the landscaper arrived. I watched as he began yanking out the dried-up weeds that he'd sprayed with Roundup several days before. Even the biggest weeds came up without a fight. It looked a lot easier than the huffing and puffing and sweating and swearing I'd endured in the front yard.

Next up was a mean-looking machine, undoubtedly a rotary tiller. As I watched, it sprang into snorting, choking, ear-splitting life. The landscaper piloted it around the backyard; it chewed up soil at an amazing speed.

I made a sandwich, rummaged around for some cookies, and reflected contentedly on my relatively bucolic morning—birds chirping, squirrels chattering, cats purring, my occasional verbal outbursts. My way was obviously superior to the monster machine method. Lunch, the *Oregonian*, and I all went into the dining room to get some peace and quiet.

By the time I was done eating, the landscaper had heaped large amounts of smelly amendments several inches thick on the backyard and was using the snorting monster to dig it in. I leaned on the sink and watched for a few minutes, then headed off for my second therapeutic bath in as many days.

When I crawled out prune-skinned an hour later, the backyard was almost completely transformed. A carpet of thick, green sod covered most of the dirt. I walked outside onto the back porch to get a closer look.

The strips of sod were bigger than I'd expected, about a foot and a half wide and maybe four feet long. They were thick, and deeply green. I was impressed in spite of myself.

"That looks nice," I said.

The landscaper looked up. "I see you put some grass seed in the front yard."

I squirmed internally. "Yeah. It was just a small spot."

He grunted. "Looks like you didn't mulch it. The birds will get the seed if you don't cover it with some bark dust or something."

"Oh, geez, that's right," I began. "I forgot all about . "

"Should have done the whole thing with sod," he rolled on, not even noticing that I was talking. "Those weeds from the other part of the lawn will just spread right over there. The grass might not sprout. You have to spend a lot of time watering it and looking after it. Sod's a lot less work." By now, he was using a huge, round drum attached to a push handle to roll the sod flat.

I contemplated a response. Should I bother to explain about the joy I was expecting when my grass seed began to glow bright green? Should I talk about the satisfaction of creating something from scratch? Should I give him a lecture on good stewardship of the earth and avoidance of toxic substances?

Naaah. I headed inside for a cup of tea and another cookie.

Chapter 4

Bulbs? What Bulbs?

For the next few weeks, I watered, and watched, and waited for the miracle of grass to occur. Every so often I saw birds hopping around and pecking at the grass seed. I let them eat.

My fancy three-tiered twine system was better at keeping me off the grass than the cats. K-word, especially, liked leaping inside the twine and running across the freshly dug dirt. We were having enough trouble trying to convince her she shouldn't sleep on the dining room table; teaching her to stay off my grass plot was probably impossible.

While waiting for the grass sprouts to show up, I kept my eye on the pansies and dusty miller and ornamental kale. The clear purple and yellow of the pansies, white of the dusty miller, and pink and purple of the kale were welcome shots of color in the mostly green and brown late autumn landscape. Every so often I got a small, warm feeling when I looked at them. *I planted flowers and they're not dying. Way to go, DesCamp.*

Within about a week, tiny green shoots of grass, almost invisible, began poking up through the bare dirt. A week after that, the shoots were tall enough to produce the green glow I'd been dreaming of when I'd begun the whole process.

"Look!" I said to Kevin one morning as he headed to the car. "It worked! It's that *green* I wanted!"

He detoured from the driveway to inspect the new grass. "Way to go! It sure is green." He gave me a quick hug and walked back to the car.

So there, I thought smugly as I waved goodbye. *Did so too work to do it from scratch.* Only one thing marred my new lawn—its uneven surface, with small hills and little depressions where water collected when I watered. Some of these dips in the ground were fairly shallow, but a few were deep enough for a cat to curl up in. It looked as if I should have paid more attention to that step about flattening the lawn with a drum roller.

Besides looking after the new grass and the winter flowers, I was also watering a clerodendrum tree—a harlequin glorybower, to be exact, the same sort of tree Therese had planted after the infamous rhubarb-in-the-front-yard episode. That clerodendrum had more than redeemed her. It was adorned in the late summer with intensely sweet-smelling white blossoms, each one surrounded by a ring of hot pink, short petal-like sepals. Come autumn, the blossoms fell off but the sepals remained, making a stunning display against the tree's metallic turquoise berries.

"Oh, good move. They're foolproof," Therese said when I told her I'd bought a clerodendrum for two dollars at a church bazaar. "The one I planted grew like crazy and was loaded with blossoms every year. And the smell!"

My clerodendrum, about twenty inches high and with four branches apparently battling for main trunk status, now resided in the large front garden bed that had held the wildflowers. Without bothering to check *Basic*, I had dug a hole, thrown in some leftover mushroom compost, plunked the tree in the dirt, and doused it with liquid fertilizer. The soil in that entire bed had just been dug and heavily amended a few weeks earlier; I couldn't imagine that it would need anything more than judicious watering and some kind words.

Therese's "foolproof" designation notwithstanding, this particular work of nature did not resemble a likely candidate for garden center-piece. On the contrary, it looked exceedingly dead. I convinced myself this was normal, given that it was nearly winter. Kevin, however, took an instant dislike to the clerodendrum and didn't hesitate to say so.

"It looks awful," he said.

"Not so loud. You'll hurt its feelings. Besides, that's what trees look like in the fall. Especially when they've just been transplanted." I dusted garden dirt off my hands onto the back of my jeans.

Kevin still looked skeptical.

"Therese's clerodendrum looked just like this after she first put it in, and it's gorgeous now," I plunged on. I was lying, of course. Her tree had never, ever looked this bad.

"Are you sure it's not dead?" Kevin persisted.

"It's nearly winter, Kevin," I snapped. "The tree is dormant. It'll be sprouting leaves and growing like crazy by next May."

"Okay, we'll give it a year."

"A year?" My voice slid up. "It's a tree, not a pansy. We'll give it as long as it needs."

"A year," he repeated. "Then if it doesn't work, I'll put a fruit tree there next fall. That's the perfect spot for a fruit tree. It gets a lot of sun."

My eyes narrowed. So *that's* why he hated my clerodendrum. "Fruit trees belong in the backyard, especially in this neighborhood. You want all those drunken thugs and the other local riff-raff to just walk right up and steal our fruit?"

"It's not that bad," Kevin protested. "There haven't been all that many thugs around. Other than that guy from around the corner," he added.

"Oh, yeah? You want to give him any excuse to come close to the house?"

"Has anything else happened since that time with Bruce?"

I shook my head. "No, not really. I've seen him ride by a couple times, but he hasn't said anything. But Kev, you don't work at home. You don't see the other scary characters parading up and down this street every day." Okay, so I was once again stretching the truth. It didn't happen every day, but at least once a week someone wandered unsteadily up the street, or burst into a loud string of profanities for no visible reason, or knocked on our front door asking if they could take our recyclable bottles, or wanted to know if they could mow our lawn. Some of these unfortunate souls bore a strong family resemblance to the bike-riding thug; most were strangers.

Kevin looked concerned. "You feel safe enough here?"

"Yeah, I guess, most of the time. But listen, I'm serious about this fruit tree, if we ever get it, staying in the backyard."

"Well, let's talk about it later." Kevin headed into the house, and I patted the clerodendrum on one of its spindly branches.

"Don't worry, I won't let him dig you up," I told it.

I watered the clerodendrum faithfully and checked it often for new signs of life. There were none. I finally decided to quit worrying and instead gave the tree little pep talks whenever I walked by. At least it didn't look any worse than when I'd planted it.

The Saturday morning after Thanksgiving, I went outside to water the new grass and encourage the clerodendrum. I picked a few small pink flowers off Cecile, who was still pumping out the blooms. Across the fence, my next-door neighbor, Mary, was hard at work in her front border. It looked as if she was planting things. Surely it was too late, even in this climate, to be putting things in the ground?

I turned off the hose and wandered over to the fence. What was she planting at this time of year?

Bulbs, that's what. Tulips. Hyacinths. Daffodils. A large box filled with small green net bags lay on the dirt beside her; each bag had five or ten bulbs inside.

"I thought I'd be smart this year and order by mail instead of rushing off to the nursery at the last minute," she said, wildly tossing bulbs into holes in the dirt. "It was a good idea, but I should have planted them six weeks ago when they arrived."

"I didn't know you could do bulbs this late," I said. "I thought they had to be in by October."

Mary sat back on her heels and looked at me. "Where'd you grow up?"

"Michigan. We did bulbs in September, October at the latest."

"Well, I grew up in Wisconsin. Same thing there. They say you can plant until the ground freezes, which some years doesn't happen at all here, but really the bulbs do better if you get them into the ground by November first. They need to get good and cold, you know. I've never put it off this long before."

"Did the guys who lived in our house have much going in the way of bulbs?" I was beginning to feel panicked. Obviously, the pansies and dusty miller weren't enough. Now I had to plant bulbs! Would this gardening grind never stop?

"They didn't have much going in the way of anything out here. Well, that's not strictly true," she corrected herself. "They reinforced that front bank with those rocks, which looked like quite a job, and then they filled in the dirt with some pretty plants. Wallflower, and some violets, and lobelia. And the ferns." She pointed down the front bank. "And that cotoneaster, and the kinnikinnick with the red berries, and some cute little succulents. And they did a good job with the wild-flowers."

"Yeah, they covered the entire backyard," I said dryly. "So the dirt and weeds didn't show."

Mary laughed. "I noticed you had sod put in. In the fifteen years I've lived here, that backyard has never been anything but dirt. It looks nice."

"Thanks," I said. "So no bulbs, hey?"

"Not many that I remember." She resumed digging and planting.

"And what about Bruce and Ed over here?"

"Yes, well, that ripped screen door says it all. They're really nice, but yard upkeep is obviously not high on their list."

"Hmmm. Yeah, I sort of got that impression." I watched her plant bulbs for a few more moments, then said goodbye.

Five minutes later, I was pulling The Fleshy One into Portland Nursery's nearly empty parking lot.

At first glance, bulbs are mysterious and complicated, not to mention downright ugly. Which end is up? How do you know what you're planting? Can something as pretty as a tulip really come from a dried-up lump that looks like a stunted onion?

A quick perusal of *Basic*'s blessedly brief section on bulbs reassured me. They're actually easy to understand, given that many things that pass for bulbs aren't actually bulbs at all. Iris and gladiolus, for instance, aren't true bulbs, although like most flowers that grow from a thickened, fleshy stem piece, they're lumped into the bulb category.

As with most plants, the main thing to remember about bulbs is to give them a good home. This means they need well-drained soil packed with nutrients, which can be a problem around Portland, where the clay dirt holds water just a little too well. Without lots of amendments dug in to lighten up the soil and improve drainage, bulbs will simply rot or, what's worse, throw up an unenthusiastic stem and a few limp leaves without producing a single bloom. This reproachful appearance reflects poorly on the human involved. "I had such potential," the plant says weakly, "but look how you've treated me." Bulbs like this let the entire world know that their caretaker is a rotten gardener and probably a bad person as well.

Besides decent soil and a good dose of daily sunlight (admittedly a major problem during soggy Portland springs), bulbs prefer to be planted right side up—a perfectly reasonable request. Fortunately for gardeners like me, the force of nature is so strong that many bulbs will grow up toward sunlight and water even if they're doing headstands in the dirt. Still, it helps to remember that, according to the illustration in *Basic*, the top end of a bulb often has a tiny stem tip poking up. The bottom is the part with hairy little root-type things sticking out. When in doubt, plunk the bulb in the ground on its broad end and pray.

As I wandered around Portland Nursery's bulb section, I reflected that at least my dirt was well-fed and ready to go. All I had to do was grab some bulbs, go home, dig holes, and drop them in.

The most grueling part of the whole ordeal would be deciding what to buy. If the pictures on the boxes were designed to make me stop, look, and drool, they worked all too well. Some of the bulb boxes were nearly empty, reminding me (as if I needed it) just how late I was. Next year, I promised myself, I would get started earlier. Maybe I'd even try mail order for my bulbs, as Mary had.

Buying by mail from a reputable bulb supplier would have been a much better way for me to shop. First, it would have slowed me down and made me think about what I was doing. I could have spent weeks, even months, lazily leafing through catalogs before committing myself to a single bulb. I could have planned for complementary colors and staggered bloom times.

Second, by planning ahead, I wouldn't have found myself poking through boxes of picked-over bulbs, searching for big, firm, healthy specimens. Instead, I'd just open a nice, sturdy shipping box and lift out strong, blemish-free bulbs, complete with planting instructions, fertilizer, and guarantees.

Third, and probably most important, given that we were on a budget with a capital "B," if I'd ordered from a catalog, I would have avoided impulse buying.

But it was too late to think about anything like that. I needed bulbs, and I needed them now: tulip, hyacinth, iris, daffodil, crocus. I grabbed the last bulb from a lily box, then put it back. Who was I kidding? I couldn't grow a lily. Lilies looked way too exotic for me, probably needed extensive care and special lily food twice a week. I looked at the terse instructions on the box. "Full or part sun. Fall plant, summer bloom. Well-drained soil. Hardy."

Hardy? Was that the horticultural equivalent of "hard to kill"? My hand crept back toward the lily box. Then I looked down at the wagon. I already had more bulbs than I could afford. Besides, I didn't know how to grow a lily. This was no time to get fancy. The lily stayed put.

I wheeled the wagon out of the bulb section and up to the cash register, where the clerk rang up nearly seventy-five dollars worth of bulbs. I gulped and began writing the check.

"Getting a late start this year, huh?" the clerk said. "You want some bulb food with these?"

Bulb food? What on earth was bulb food? Of course I wanted bulb food.

"I was looking for it back there, but didn't see it," I lied.

"Bottom shelf, just under the tulips."

"Uh, right. Thanks." I walked back to the tulips and snagged a box of bulb food. As I straightened up, I spotted a box with a picture of a spectacular tulip—nearly black, tall, stately. I grabbed one bulb and scurried back to the cash register. If I didn't get out of here, I wouldn't be able to afford a trip to Starbucks until well after the first bulb poked up through the dirt.

According to my box of bulb food, newly planted bulbs should be fed twice a year—in the fall when they're planted, and in the spring just as they begin to bloom. In succeeding years, bulbs should be fed only once, after the flowers have faded. This is when bulbs have depleted almost all of their stored-up food and must recover some energy in order to produce strong blooms the following spring. *Basic* states that the regenerative process happens most effectively when the gardener stays out of Mother Nature's way and lets the leaves remain on the plant until they're completely yellow and withered. During this time, the leaves take in light energy from the sun, manufacture food, and replenish the bulbs' energy reserves. In other words, after you plant bulbs, you can pretty much ignore them for most of the year. This is my sort of flower.

Bulb food itself is made up of those good old garden standbys—nitrogen, phosphorus, and potassium—along with calcium and whatever other goodies each bulb-food manufacturer decides to include.

Slug Tossing

My bulb food contained, according to the box, "Nine key nutrients and micronutrients." Some of the micronutrients were micro, indeed: iron, manganese, and molybdenum came in at well under one percent of the total mix. *Like this is going to make a difference to the bulb*, I thought skeptically as I read the list of ingredients. But I'd bought the stuff, and I was going to use it.

I arrived home with seven brown paper bags full of spring hope, grabbed my battered hand fork, and set to work. Not for me the stiff, neat rows of tulips marching across the front of the house. I decided instead to try something I'd seen Therese do—strew the bulbs across the bed at random, then plant them where they fell. In gardening terms, this is called naturalizing, because, if done with a large enough quantity of bulbs, it produces closely massed drifts of flowers that look as if they've grown and multiplied naturally over the years. In my book, however, it's called laziness. I could just toss bulbs into the dirt and not worry about lining them up in straight lines or bringing order to the process.

Walking along the front garden bed, I used the same arm motion that I'd employed for broadcasting grass seed—arm sweeping back and forth—with the same awkward results. Instead of bulbs falling gracefully from my outstretched hand, they tumbled down in spurts and dribbles. Several bulbs fell right on top of the pansies, others landed a little too close to the clerodendrum. One potential tulip landed in the middle of an ornamental kale. Obviously, a little judicious cheating was in order here. I rearranged the bulbs and fretted over the many bare spots. Seventy-five bucks worth of bulbs barely made a dent in my naked garden beds. Did I have the time to head back to the nursery for more bulbs? Yes. Did I have the money? No. I stayed put and began digging holes, adding a little bulb food to the bottom of each hole, then plopping the bulb on top of the mixture of bulb food and dirt.

Just as I finished, Kevin arrived home from his Saturday morning martial arts workout. "What are you doing now?" he asked, getting out of the car with a puzzled look on his face.

"Bulbs," I said.

"You mean like tulips? You can plant them this late?"

"Oh, yeah." I spoke with the obnoxious self-assurance of the new expert. "You can plant them until the ground freezes over. Although this is a *little* late. But they'll be okay."

He took in the neatly smoothed dirt of the garden bed, the pansies and dusty miller and ornamental kale, and then me with my dirty hands. "Thanks for doing all this work. You're turning into a regular gardener."

"Good God, I hope not," I said, horrified. "I have better things to do with my time."

Chapter 5

Oh, the Weather Outside Is Frightful . . .

*I*t was raining.

Of course it was raining. In late January, in Portland, Oregon, what else would it be doing?

The rain shredded the soft pansy petals. It turned the big garden bed into a murky, muddy brown sea on which floated pansies and dusty miller and kale, all past their prime and sagging sideways. It pounded down so hard that puddles formed in the little depressions left from my November bulb-planting spree. I thought I'd raked the soil pretty flat after I planted the bulbs. But then, I thought I'd flattened the soil in the little bit of lawn I'd seeded, too, and that area still resembled a large-scale relief map.

January didn't just feature rain in ark-producing quantities. It also brought my near-annual case of bronchitis. On the first day of my illness, Kevin went to the pharmacy to pick up some Vicks VapoRub (which had been a staple of my childhood) and my prescription cough syrup. He came home with . . .

"*ValuRub?*" I croaked in disbelief. "I don't want some cheap imitation stuff. I want Vicks."

"Sweetie, I read the ingredients list. It's exactly the same." He unscrewed the jar and waved it under my nose. "See? It smells just like Vicks."

I started to cry. "It *doesn't*. I'm *sick*. I want *Vicks*."

He went back to the store and brought home the real thing, by which time I was feeling incredibly silly but still adamant. After all, this was the man who paid someone else to mow our lawn. How could he even consider buying a cheap version of mentholated chest rub?

"I'm sorry about the ValuRub," he said, smearing Vicks on my chest and under my nose. "I guess I'm just a low-cost value hub."

"No, you're a great hubbo." I barked out the biggest cough I could muster and tried my best to look pale and sickly, which wasn't hard. "And not so low cost, either. But some things are sacred."

Now, two weeks later, still coughing, I hunched over my morning mug of tea and stared out the living room windows at the mud puddles in the garden beds and thought about my seventy-five dollars worth of bulbs rotting in the water-logged soil. Not much I could do about it now but wait for spring and hope the bulbs survived.

We'd had a wonderfully busy first holiday season in the little blue house. I'd thrown a big surprise party for Kevin's early December birthday; friends and family had spilled throughout the house (and, not surprisingly, spilled wine on the already unattractive kitchen carpet). The week before Christmas brought a wild party next door at Bruce and Ed's, with nearly a hundred people packed into their tiny house. We met neighbors we'd previously only waved at and chatted with the people who lived across the backyard fence. I spent a long time talking with Connie, the violist, after we discovered a mutual interest in underwater photography—she took pictures while scuba diving; I've always been fascinated by such shots. The party reinforced what Kevin had said all along—that this neighborhood was, after all, a pretty good spot with pretty good people.

Christmas Eve brought an ice storm and the postponement of our plans to spend time with our families. On Christmas morning, I picked a small bouquet of pansies and put them in a slim crystal vase on the dining room table. We built a huge fire and kept it going all day. That night, we walked up to Peacock Lane. As it is each December, the one-block stretch of small homes was completely covered with Christmas lights and front-lawn displays of Santa and reindeer and Baby Jesus and the Three Wise Men. Carols poured out onto the cold night air from elaborate speaker systems. People streamed up and down the sidewalks. A steady parade of cars and vans packed with sightseers drove down the street. One of the vans had a small fir tree, complete with blinking lights, wired to its front grill. The whole scene was an amazing mix of pretty and tacky. I wasn't quite sure what to make of it.

"They do this for two whole weeks?" I said as we walked the four blocks back to our house.

"Yeah, for like thirty or forty years they've done it," Kevin said. "We used to come here when I was a kid. Think of the electricity bills."

After the bright lights of Peacock Lane, Southeast Alder Street was dark and eerie. We held hands and slid home on the icy sidewalks.

And now the holidays were over. That familiar post-holiday letdown lasted a little longer than usual this year. We'd come home from a weekend trip to the beach to find that Ed, wildly dramatic Ed, incredibly social Ed, had collapsed of a heart attack during a dinner party.

Bruce brought the news over after we got home. He stood sobbing in our living room and told us, "He was waving a glass of wine in the air and carrying on and all of a sudden he just sat down. It's how he'd want to go, really—surrounded by friends, giving a party."

We hugged Bruce and wondered how to help. For all his flair and flash, Ed had seemed like the one who was in charge. Connie and Kevin and I talked about Bruce and worried about him. We had him over for dinner. I took him homemade bread and hounded him about whether he was eating well (he wasn't) and whether he was smoking too much (he was).

And it kept raining.

At least the rain gave me a good excuse to stay inside, warm, dry, and far away from garden chores. All of that nonsense was done for the time being. Leaves had been raked and bagged, grass seed and sod were well established, bulbs were planted, and the clerodendrum was—well, it didn't look completely dead. I figured I had at least a month before the first weeds showed up and made me feel guilty, and another two weeks after that before the guilt actually drove me to do any work.

This particular morning was as gray and dreary as the ones before it, and the ones that would undoubtedly follow. I glared out the kitchen window at the gray skies and wished myself back in California instead of stuck here in this damp, moldy, wrung-out old dishcloth of a town. I heaved a huge sigh and headed back into my study, where I was greeted by a blank computer screen and a fuzzy gray and white kitten sleeping on top of the computer.

This fluffball was the latest addition to our family. I'd found her two months earlier, meowing under a truck parked across the street. She was cold, quivering, scared, and hungry. Kevin was out of town on a business trip, and I didn't waste time negotiating over the phone about adopting a third cat. Instead, I showed her a bowl of cat food and lured her across Alder Street to our sheltered front porch, where a wooden fruit crate stuffed with old towels and pillows awaited. The cat food dish went next to the fruit crate. She took to her new home immediately. My plan was to let her stay outside for a few days, then bring her inside when Pug and K-word had gotten used to having her around.

"We are *not* having three cats," Kevin said when he arrived home the next evening.

"Please?" I begged. "Look at the poor thing."

He looked. "We have too many vet bills as it is."

"But she needs a home." I started to sniffle. I was already hopelessly in love with the newcomer. "She'll starve. And she's so sweet. Just *look* at her."

Kevin looked again. He scratched her between the ears and a huge rumbly purr arose. A smile tugged at the corners of his mouth. "Well—okay, but she'll have to live on the front porch. No more indoor kitties."

"What? It's winter. It's cold. She'll freeze to death."

"Meg. She has *fur*. She's a *cat*. She'll be *fine*."

I sniffed loudly and went inside to fetch another helping of cat food.

Two weeks later, on a cold, wet, windy night, I was curled up on the couch reading. Kevin went out to the car to get something. When he came back, he had the fluffball cat in his arms and a sheepish expression on his face.

"It's so cold," he said simply.

So now we had three cats. We named the new family member Whoo, and after a few hissing matches with K-word, she settled right in, claiming the warm top of my computer as her special place.

Right now, however, the computer wasn't as warm as it should be. It was ten o'clock, and I hadn't yet settled down to the day's work.

Maybe a little winter gardening wasn't such a bad idea, I thought, thumbing through my to-do file (call an editor, write a pitch letter, draft an article outline). At least it would get me away from this stuff.

"This stuff" was my attempt to crack the national magazine market, something I worked at whenever my project load from local clients was low. I'd wrapped up a series of newsletters and brochures right before Christmas, and now had free time to hound my list of New York–based magazine editors.

My emotions went up and down wildly as I pursued national projects. Some days I was obscenely optimistic about my prospects for success (after all, people write for major publications all the time; sooner or later I would do so as well, right?). Other days, the odds, which were overwhelmingly against me, made me wish I were a software engineer, or a kindergarten teacher, or a long-distance trucker.

Anything would be better than facing rejection day in and day out.

I put down my to-do file and stared forlornly at the computer screen as I stroked Whoo's fur.

I needed to *do* something.

Just then someone knocked on the door. I fled my office, glad of the distraction.

One of the brothers from around the corner stood on the porch. It wasn't the one who'd yelled at Bruce and me, so I opened the door.

"Hi. Got any bottles I can have?"

"Sorry," I said. "We don't drink pop or anything like that."

"Okay." He stumped off the porch. I watched him bypass Bruce's house and head up Connie's front walk. "He came over once when I was having a dinner party and said if I'd give him ten dollars, he'd mow the lawn the next day," Connie had told me once. "I told him he could mow the lawn the next day but I wouldn't pay him until it was done."

Now, I watched him with a mixture of annoyance and sorrow and guilt. What sort of life did he have, part of a family known as the neighborhood bad guys, going from door to door looking for returnable bottles? This guy probably faced more rejection in a single week than I had in three years as a freelance writer. Then I thought about Bruce and Ed and felt even worse.

I made a fresh mug of tea, then sank down on the dirty kitchen carpet and looked across the room at the glass-fronted built-in china cabinet. After brooding for ten minutes on my relatively cushy life and my inability to kick start myself into editor-hounding gear, the answer to my inactivity and foul mood presented itself.

I would paint the kitchen.

New paint wouldn't disguise the old linoleum on the countertops, or the horrid carpet, or make a garbage disposal appear under the sink. But it was easy—far easier than trying to convince some snooty Manhattan editor that I was exactly what her readers had been waiting for. I looked around the purple kitchen one last time, then jumped in The Fleshy One and drove to the paint store.

When Kevin came home that night and saw the paint chips taped to the walls, I saw him go into controlled breathing mode. "Oh," he said pleasantly. "We're painting?"

"No," I assured him. "I'm painting."

"What about work?"

I shrugged and avoided his eyes. "No work out there right now. And besides, the house really needs some help. Plus, I want to paint in here before we rip the carpet out."

"My mom used to work inside the house during the winter, too," Kevin said, rummaging in the refrigerator. "That and look at gardening catalogs."

"Really?" I felt a surprising little surge of interest. Looking at catalogs, even gardening catalogs, would be a good way to kill some time. "Where'd she get them?"

He shrugged, his head still in the refrigerator. "Didn't we have some salsa?"

"Second shelf, in the back," I said automatically. "Where'd she get the catalogs?" I repeated.

"Who knows? They just came, I think." He took a bag of tortilla chips from their resting place in a basket on top of the refrigerator.

"I'm gonna make a phone call," I said.

"Well, let's see," Therese said. "I guess I get a catalog from Breck's, and one from a rose nursery in California, and Schreiner's—you know, that iris place in Salem—and I don't know who all else."

"I know Schreiner's," I said. "I used to write copy for their brochures. So, you still have any catalogs around?"

"No, I think I recycled everything after I placed my order," she said. "But you could call information for their toll-free numbers and then order the catalogs. Hey, you must really be getting into gardening if you're thinking of it during the dead of winter. You know this is a good time of year to pull weeds, when it's really wet out. The roots come out really easily during the winter. I go out every so often and just check on things, pull some weeds if I see any."

"Yeah, and you get bronchitis from being out in the rain. No thanks. Been there already." I coughed as hard as I could.

"Wimp."

"Masochist."

"Whatever. Talk to you later."

"Yeah." I hung up the phone and looked out my office window at the front yard. Were weeds already growing in my garden beds? Did I care if they were? Good thing it was too dark to see. Maybe I'd look tomorrow.

And maybe not.

Chapter 6

Slug Tossing

There is, I am convinced, a force in the universe whose sole function is to wreak havoc upon the words spoken by two people in a long-term relationship. You speak, the force acts, and what your mate hears is something different from what you said. Maybe a little different, maybe a lot different. But different enough to add excitement, confusion, frustration to your relationship.

That force was why our paint-spotted carpet remained our paint-spotted carpet for months after I'd painted the kitchen. I thought we had agreed to replace the carpet immediately after painting the kitchen. Kevin thought we'd agreed to do it when we had the money.

I worked off my frustration with more painting. The dark brown hallway, which had sucked up light like a black hole, was now soft cream. Light from the living room and my office gleamed off the new paint. Little by little, the house was coming together.

Which was more than I could say for myself. The dark and cold and rain of January turned into the dark and cold and rain of February. My mood plummeted with each new storm front. Late one Sunday morning, as I contemplated the travel section in the newspaper and tried to figure out how we could afford a trip to the tropics (we could sell the car, we could sell the house, we could sell the cats to someone interested in studying the properties of inertia), the sun appeared. I pulled on an extra sweater and my red rubber rain boots and went out to walk around the yard.

Once outside, I found a pleasant surprise: the first signs of spring. Green shoots an inch or two tall were pushing through the mud in the garden beds. I took a tour of the front yard, bending down to look at each stem and marvel at what my last-minute raid on the nursery had accomplished.

Another sign of spring was the sorry condition of my winter flowers. The kale, dusty miller, and pansies were leggy and tattered. It was past time to pull them out, and I did so with a light heart, knowing that blooming bulbs couldn't be far behind. Some of the pansy petals had little half-moon indentations at the edges. I puzzled over this, finally deciding that rain must have caused the damage. I'd blamed rain for a lot of things in the past; this was just something to add to the list.

The rest of the winter wasn't so bad. Every few days, I roamed around the garden for five or ten minutes, taking inventory. It was obvious that the soil needed more work; even with all of last fall's digging, the muddy garden dirt still betrayed its heavy, thick, clay nature. But the plants continued to grow and took on more definite shapes. It looked like my dirt-digging, bulb-buying frenzy would pay off.

After a few more weeks and a visit from Therese, I could tentatively identify most of the plants by their foliage: Tulips had the broad leaves, hyacinth grew in a sort of circle of leaves, dwarf iris leaves were skinny. The remainder were slender-leafed daffodils.

Unfortunately, the plants had other close observers.

"So, are the slugs making you crazy?" Therese asked as we stood on the sidewalk admiring the emerging plants.

"Slugs? Don't have 'em, as far as I know."

"This is Portland, Meg. Everyone has slugs, especially this time of year." She bent down and turned over a dead maple leaf that lay in the nearby garden bed. "See?" An extended slug family had set up house-keeping under this cozy retreat. "And see this?" She pointed to ragged leaf edges on a daffodil. "Slugs. And this half-chewed stem? Ick." She picked a slug off the stem of a hyacinth, dropped the slimy critter on the sidewalk, and stepped on him.

I stared in horror, not sure which was more appalling, slugs attacking my precious plants or squished slug bodies on my front walk.

"You can tell by the trails they leave, too," Therese went on. I turned around and looked where she was pointing. Sure enough, silvery trails of slime crisscrossed the beds and the front walkway.

"Good God. Do they eat tulips?" I asked in horror, thinking of the big, black tulip I was waiting to see sprout and bloom.

"They eat just about anything, especially bulbs." Therese shrugged. "You could use beer. Elizabeth always does."

"Yuk. That's awful. They drown."

"Yes, they do drown," she said. "You could try spraying on some insecticidal soap, but it's never worked for us."

Therese left, but not before pointing out nibble spots on more of my daffodils. I stood in the garden reflecting on slugs. They must have been responsible for the half-moon edges on the pansies. A more experienced gardener would have expected slugs—Portland is nearly as famous for slugs as it is for roses and rhododendrons—but I had totally overlooked the likelihood that they would munch my flowers. Slugs seemed sort of like a social disease. They might happen to other people, but not to me.

Yet there they were, attacking my expensive bulbs. This meant war.

I marched into the garage, grabbed a trowel and a plastic bag, and marched back to the front garden beds. Thirty minutes of frenzied scooping yielded more slugs than I ever imagined could gather in one place. I closed my mind against the thought that maybe I was depriving living beings of a meaningful life; I jammed the bag into the garbage can and I clanged the lid on. *That* would teach them. The few slugs who'd escaped my wrath would spread the word, and they'd all stay out of my garden for the rest of the year.

The next morning, of course, I found more slugs.

Given the right conditions (and oh, does Portland ever have them), slugs are incredibly prolific. They're like the rhythm-method practitioners of the mollusk world, with predictable results: A single great gray garden slug can lay up to five hundred fertile eggs each year.

This drive to thrive takes place not just in lab-controlled conditions, where it's relatively easy to count how many eggs a slug produces, but in the wild as well. Scientifically based rumor, as reported in David George Gordon's *Field Guide to the Slug*, has it that an English zoologist spent several years collecting and disposing of four hundred slugs *each night* from a single quarter-acre garden. This gives rise to many questions: How can anything possibly reproduce that fast? Given that they do, why do we even try to control them? And most importantly, what sort of person would spend every night for several years rooting slugs out of the dirt? Obviously this person, who is no doubt a very nice, if perhaps somewhat *different* sort of guy, found slugs interesting. There's a name for people like this (well, probably several names in varying degrees of politeness): malacologist.

Malacology is a branch of zoology dealing with the mollusk phylum, some members of which many people consider quite yummy—clams, oysters, snails. Then there's the far-less-toothsome slug.

Some malacologists, such as the above-mentioned Englishman, spend their entire careers watching slugs. They hold advanced degrees in slug studies and write long, footnoted papers about slugs that are published in academic journals. Like other scholars, they probably engage in heated debates sparked by controversial articles. The furious round of letters to the editor is easy to imagine: "As any beginning zoology student knows, but the author of 'Wild Slugs, Wild Mushrooms' has grievously forgotten, the reticulated *Prophysaon andersoni* prefers chanterelle mushrooms, not psilocybe . . ." "With all due respect to my learned colleague, based on my extensive and rigorous laboratory studies as outlined in Volume XXI, Issue XVIII, of this journal, the reticulated *P. andersoni* has been shown to prefer the psilocybe mushroom when given a choice . . ."

Which leads me to wonder just how much taxpayer money is going to fund slug research. We're talking here about a squishy, slimy critter with a really high yuk factor, 27,000 teeth (yes, per slug mouth), green blood, and the ability to mate with itself should the need arise. That last attribute alone should be enough to get the social conservatives up in arms.

Even though most people find them disgusting, slugs undoubtedly don't care. They must think they've found a little piece of heaven here in the Pacific Northwest. The area provides, in obscene excess, the three things slugs need in order to flourish: abundant plant life, moisture, and soil with at least some trace of volcanic activity. You can just see the head slug in a herd of immigrating great grays arriving at the Oregon border, waving its eyeball stalk at the scenery, and shouting back to the rest of the crew, "This is it, guys! Unpack the trunks."

The slug that Northwest gardeners fight most often is the great gray garden slug. At just four inches, this slug makes up in speed (well, relatively speaking) what it lacks in length. Great grays can crawl up to four times faster than the banana slug, which clocks in at about 32.5 feet per hour on a good day. ("I wish I could remember more," the banana slug told the police after being mugged by two great grays. "But it all happened so fast.")

The great gray has another characteristic besides its speediness: It's a cannibal. Yes, these charming creatures actually attack and eat other slugs, mostly the gentle, nonaggressive native slugs. This is where its speed comes in most handy, sort of like a cheetah in an all-out sprint chasing its next meal across the plains of Africa. Most slugs, however, are happy to munch vegetation rather than each other.

The morning after I thought I'd cleared all the slugs from my garden, I took a reconnaissance tour and found more slugs. Slug trails wound through the garden beds and led to clever hiding spots—under tulip leaves, under the winter pansies, under the top row of flat rocks lining the steep side of the flower border. Where had they come from? How could I get rid of them? This called for research, rather than action. I left the slugs where they were and retreated inside to a cup of tea and *Basic*.

Apparently, I had three options: I could bait the garden with poison, set up slug hotels filled with beer, or commit myself to spending a half hour each morning pawing through the dirt looking for slugs. More out of curiosity than in search of a solution, I turned to the section on poisons.

Metaldehyde was listed as the poison of choice for slugs and snails. It's related to methanol, or wood alcohol. "Be careful with metaldehyde mixed with bran; it's highly poisonous to birds and pets," the book warned. Highly attractive, as well. That wasn't very comforting. I scanned the general discussion about chemicals. The warnings continued: Wash your hands and other exposed skin. Wash any clothing that comes in contact with the poison. Store it under lock and key.

There's good reason for all the caution. Metaldehyde doesn't just dispatch slugs and snails; it can seriously harm the human nervous system, even cause death at the right dose. Much smaller amounts, of course, can harm or kill birds and small mammals—squirrels, raccoons, my cats.

Other popular slug-bait ingredients include carbamate compounds and methiocarb. Both are more toxic than metaldehyde. Methiocarb should never be used around the home gardener's veggie plot (or any commercial grower's food crop, for that matter), and carbamates are so strong they kill off earthworms, the most welcome workers in any garden.

Now, I'm not a granola head with a different Guatemalan string bag for every social occasion and a fierce dedication to a meat-free lifestyle, but I do think it's important to leave the earth a little better, rather than a little worse, from my gardening efforts. And I was still feeling miffed about the use of herbicides in our backyard last fall. So chemical poisons were not an option for my garden beds.

There had to be something else that would work. On Therese's advice, I went to the main branch of the Multnomah County Library and paged through back issues of *Organic Gardening* magazine, looking for a solution.

Boy, did I find them.

Nonchemical slug controls are like recipes for meatloaf: Everyone and his Aunt Fanny has one they swear by. Many of these favorite solutions are barrier methods. One of the most common is spreading diatomaceous earth (clay kitty litter) or bark dust around susceptible plants. The idea is that as slugs crawl over the sharp-edged particles, they'll be cut to smithereens, all their bodily fluids will seep out, and they'll dehydrate. Presto! Dead slug. However, given that your basic-issue slime-encased slug can crawl along the edge of a razor blade or cross a pile of glass shards without sustaining any damage, I find it hard to believe that kitty litter would be effective.

Another barrier method is to sink wide copper bands into the ground. The theory behind this is that slugs who touch the bands will receive a mild electric shock, turn around, and head into your neighbor's yard. This method is supposed to work well, but those copper bands don't come cheap. And I needed cheap.

I called Therese.

"Hey, what was that about beer and slugs?"

"Sink a kitty food can or a cottage cheese container into the ground and pour in some beer at night. Then check it the next morning. Sometimes the cottage cheese container is best because you can cut a little hole in the lid, put the lid on, and if it rains the beer won't get diluted."

"Right." I shuddered. Visions of soggy, limp slug bodies flashed in front of my eyes. "Anything else?"

"Some people use salt. I think if you're close enough to salt them, you might as well just pick them up and toss them in the garbage. What's left, metaldehyde? We don't use it, but I guess it works."

Trust Therese to know what the appropriate poison was even if she wasn't using it.

"Nope, no metaldehyde here either," I said. "Thanks anyway." I heard a confused babble on the other end of the line. "What?"

"Hang on," Therese said.

I hung on. A new voice came across the phone lines. It was our friend Julia. "Meg? Wanna know how my grandmother Julia

Zumstein handled slugs?"

"Of course."

"You know she lived on the coast in Tillamook and had a huge garden? Well, she'd go out in her garden every morning, wearing a housedress, an apron, high-top black Converse All-Stars, and a sombrero, and she'd pick up the slugs and fling them into her incinerator."

"No way!"

"I'm serious. And she was the sweetest woman who ever lived. Something about slugs brought out the beast in her."

I hung up and contemplated sweet, gentle Julia Zumstein in her sombrero. Too bad we didn't have an incinerator.

So far, I'd consulted two reference books, a stack of magazines, and two real live people, and I still didn't have an acceptable way to deal with my slug problem. Poisons were out; drowning seemed cruel; salting seemed even crueler. Salted slugs literally dehydrate to death, and with a slug's multitude of nerve endings, salting makes for a particularly painful death.

What was left? All the time-consuming, up-close-and-personal methods I'd hoped to avoid: Picking slugs out of the dirt and putting them in the garbage. Leaving out overturned grapefruit rinds and capturing the slugs that crawled inside. Putting one board on top of another, inserting a small pebble in between to make enough space for slugs to snuggle up in, then removing the pebble and stomping on the boards (and, indirectly, the slugs). None of these methods appealed to me. I wanted to avoid being directly responsible for the demise of their sluggy souls, and I also didn't want to be funeral director for their slimy corpses.

The next morning, I ventured outside again. More slugs. More nibbles out of plants. My black tulip, which had bloomed just days before, had bite marks on its leaves. I spotted a slug climbing the stem of a healthy hyacinth. Without thinking, I reached down, plucked it off, and hurled it into the street. "Just try to get back here, you rotten slug, you," I muttered, and looked around for another. Ten minutes later, I was still hunting and slinging. A little light had gone on in my brain: If I threw the slugs into the street, I wasn't really causing their deaths, was I? They'd be eaten by a bird, or run over by a car, or dried up by the sun. They'd be dead, all right, but I wouldn't have to actually dance on their bodies or lure them to a fatal beer swim.

Add to this the sheer physical gratification of ripping slugs off my plants and flinging them as hard as I could into the street, and I was convinced I'd found the best way to deal with the pests. It might be time intensive, but it was intensely satisfying. I finally headed inside, flushed with victory.

"What are you doing?" Kevin asked curiously as I stood at the sink, washing and washing and washing my hands.

I grimaced. "Trying to get the slug slime off."

"Oh." There was a brief silence, then, "And why are you covered with slug slime?"

"Because I've been tossing slugs into the street."

"Okay." Another pause. "And why were you slug tossing?"

I explained my thoughts on slug removal. Always ready for a debate about ethics and philosophy, Kevin jumped right in.

"So you're removing them from their natural habitat and tossing them into the street, but you think you're not really killing them?

That's not very logical, Weglet. You're responsible for their deaths, even if you don't actually do the killing yourself."

"That's not true," I protested, finally giving up on the soap and water. I reached for a hand towel, rubbed off the remaining slime, and tossed the towel down the laundry chute. "They're going to be eaten by a bird or squashed by a car. I'm not doing it."

"But the bird or car wouldn't get them if you didn't first toss them into the street," he said stubbornly. "You're just as guilty of killing those slugs as if you poisoned them." He looked at his watch. "Gotta go. By the way, next time you're covered with slug slime, just rub your hands together. It rolls up like glue and you can just peel it off. Slug slime absorbs water. That's why it's so hard to wash off."

"Really? Where'd you learn that?"

He shrugged. "I don't remember. Just one of those things you learn when you grow up here."

"Hey, you mean you knew that all this time and yet you watched me washing my hands for five minutes?"

"You make a good Lady Macbeth," he said as he picked up his briefcase.

"I'll feed you slugs for dinner if you're not careful," I yelled at his back as he went out the front door.

Slugs for dinner isn't such a crazy idea. After all, there's a thin line between slug and snail. More accurately, there's a thin shell between the two creatures. For many people, that shell is enough to justify treating the slug's cousin as a culinary delight. The rest of us see the snail for what it is: a slug in drag.

I ate my first and last snails while visiting Quebec City as a freshman in high school. Everything about those snails is permanently burned into my memory: The little clay pot they arrived in, the tiny-tined, long-handled fork I used to pry them from their shells, the candle burning under the melted butter. And then the snails themselves: Small. Wild tasting. Chewy. Make that *very* chewy. This was gourmet dining? As I chomped and swallowed and tried to look nonchalant, I realized for the first time that enough garlic and melted butter can make anything palatable, even fashionable.

Now, after waging a long campaign of war against the snail's cousin, I know I'll never eat another snail. The vision of 27,000 teeth, green blood, and that all-encompassing coat of slime would be ever before me as I coaxed snail bodies from their shells.

Not even butter and garlic can disguise some things.

Chapter 7

But I Don't Like Roses

Living in Portland brings with it a unique civic duty: growing roses. This is, after all, the self-proclaimed City of Roses, complete with an annual Rose Festival that includes a grass-trashing carnival at downtown's Waterfront Park, at least three traffic-snarling parades, and a media-savvy bevy of Rose Princesses culled from local high schools. If you have any doubt about Portland's affinity for roses, or vice versa, just check *Sunset Western Garden Book*: "Any mention of the Willamette Valley must include roses . . . which attain near perfection here."

All of which makes it tough on someone like me who doesn't particularly like roses.

The first year I lived in Portland, my sisters dragged me to the Grand Floral Parade, an extravaganza that rivals Macy's Thanksgiving

Day Parade. Elizabeth, Therese, and their friends had the parade-watching drill down. A few brave souls hit the parade route at seven in the morning armed with blankets, lawn chairs, thermoses of coffee, bags of croissants, and the morning paper. Their mission was to stake out prime curb space. By the time the rest of us joined them at ten o'clock, the streets were packed for blocks around, even though it was fifty-five degrees and threatening to rain.

"Typical Rose Festival parade weather," someone remarked.

"Then why are we here?" I asked, shivering over my third cup of coffee and desperately trying to spot a portable toilet. "This is on TV, right?" No one answered. They were all too busy doing the beauty-queen wave—elbow, elbow, wrist, wrist. I tried, too, and spilled coffee on my shoes. Just then, it started to pour. Umbrellas popped open up and down the street. I pulled up the hood of my slicker and tried to remember why I'd moved to this God-forsaken city and why I was hanging out with my sisters.

I've never been very fond of roses, but that first Rose Festival parade experience almost completely wiped out any possibility that roses would ever find a place in my heart—or my garden. Most roses require far too much work for what they give back: tough, thorny stems, bugs and black spot and rust. A garden of roses means hours inspecting, pruning, spraying, worrying, spraying again. I had better things to do with my small amount of gardening time.

But I also had a husband who is a Portland native. Kevin loves roses. Kevin, as I found out one April morning, wanted roses.

"But I don't *like* roses," I protested. "They're thorny. They're hard to grow. Plus they're ugly nine months out of the year."

"You like that little pink bush in the front yard," he reminded me. "You were picking roses off it until November of last year, remember?"

"That's Cecile," I said. "That's different. She's old. She smells good. And she's tough. She's been around forever, and I bet no bug has ever dared to even look at her."

"Well, there's no reason our roses can't be tough, too. Besides, my mom grew roses when I was growing up. If we have them here, it will make it feel more like a home to me." He had that look I'd come to recognize—the look that meant he was ready to argue—or, rather, *discuss*—until we were both blue in the face.

After nearly four years of marriage, I was finally beginning to realize when something was worth arguing about and when it was better to just give in. If Kevin thought roses would make our little place more homey, then by golly, he could have his roses. But, in return, I bargained for plants that I wanted: four rhododendrons, a winter-blooming daphne, lily-of-the-valley for the shady rock garden, a lilac bush. Memories of the two huge lilac borders in our Michigan yard filled my head. I could practically smell the blossoms—much more enticing than that overexposed rose fragrance.

"Okay, so we get the roses. Just remember I don't want anything to do with them," I warned him.

"Don't worry. I'll take care of it."

When Kevin says he'll take care of something, he takes care of it. That weekend, we went to Portland Nursery. I wandered around looking at lilacs and rhododendrons and daphne, filling a wagon with pansies and petunias, and trying in vain to find lily-of-the-valley, only to discover they have to be planted in the fall. Kevin spent nearly two hours picking out half a dozen rosebushes and arranging for their delivery. He examined the tags hanging from the bushes, talked with nursery personnel, and made his decisions based on a combination of common sense and emotional reaction. As we drove home, he described the roses he'd picked—lavender, white, apricot, red. I had to admit they sounded pretty.

At home, we unloaded Kevin's other purchases—strawberry plants and tomato plants, packets of corn and pepper seeds, a big box of rose food, and a big box of rhododendron food, which could also be used on the azaleas. I read the instructions on the side of the box. "Feed in the spring just before or just after flowering, then monthly until end of summer." Sounded easy enough. Maybe I'd use some on the azalea hedge, which was starting to burst into incredible mounds of bright pink blossoms. It might not be the perfect time to feed them, but food at the wrong time was probably better than no food at all.

We stood in the front yard, surveying the planting area for the roses and rhododendrons.

"I'm not sure the roses will get enough sunlight against that west fence," Kevin said. "The guy at the nursery said they need at least six hours of sun each day."

I took a deep breath. "They'll get that much."

"Yeah, well, I described our yard and he said they'd do best with that southern exposure right across the front of the house."

I could feel my jaw harden. "I want a year-round hedge of green against the house, not a bunch of thorny rosebushes."

He didn't answer.

"Please?"

"You really think they'll get enough sunlight against that fence?" he asked.

"Yeah, I really think so. And if they don't, we'll transplant them. I promise."

"Okay. And we'll put the rhodies and the lilac in the front, where you want them." As we walked into the house, he said casually, "Oh, I got two fruit trees, too."

"Fruit trees, huh? For the backyard, right?"

"Right, unless . . ."

"No. Keep your mitts off my clerodendrum." Next year, I told myself, I would get this stuff in writing. We didn't need a prenuptial agreement, which we were too late for, anyway. We needed a pre-planting agreement.

When Kevin and I were planning our wedding, I gave the florist just two rules: No baby's breath and no roses. Anything else was open for discussion.

I am clearly out of step with the mainstream on this issue. Roses are undoubtedly the most popular flower in the United States, perhaps in the entire world. It's not just that they smell good (usually) and look good (if they're pampered). They also have a romantic lineage that adds to their glory and charm. Hundreds, probably thousands, of songs and poems over the centuries have extolled the glory of the rose and the glory of the loved one who is just like the rose. Rose milk, rose petals, walled rose gardens, rose windows in grand European cathedrals, *sub rosa* meetings in Roman times (where a rose hanging from the room's ceiling indicated that the gathering was to be kept secret). The rose is rampant in history and popular culture.

Roses have played their part in wars, as well, most obviously England's War of the Roses. There are other wartime rose sagas: Josephine searched out new roses from countries that Napoleon was busy conquering; cuttings of the then new, now ubiquitous Peace rose made it out of France on the last plane to leave before the Nazis rolled in.

Even a cynic like me has to admit that it's hard to beat the rose for history and excitement.

Today the flower is still used to invoke visions of beauty, but in brazenly commercial ways. Roses run riot at the cosmetics counters in every department store: Red Rose lipstick, Sheer Rose blusher, rose-tinted and rose-monikered eyeshadow and nail polish. The poetic lyricism of the past has given way to the sales-driven creative flights of the advertising copywriter.

Because of all this, roses have become a floral and cultural cliché. What, according to the florist industry, is the ultimate romantic present for Valentine's Day? A dozen long-stemmed roses, of course. What do unimaginative dueling sweeties send each other after a fight? Uh-huh—twelve of the finest. What did my college boyfriend send me after I dumped him? Yup.

If he'd sent lilacs, I might have considered taking him back.

"He wants to grow roses," I confided to Therese over a decaf grande no-whip mocha at the Starbucks on Hawthorne Boulevard.

She took a sip of her latte (grande, extra foam, all the caffeine, please). "What's wrong with roses? This is the perfect climate for them."

"That's just it." I took a bite of a shortbread cookie and looked out the window at the parade of shoppers and slackers. "*Everyone* has roses here. I don't see what's so great about them. And it seems like they're an awful lot of work."

"You'll do fine," she assured me.

"No, *he'll* do fine. I told him he had to take care of the roses."

"I thought you did the flowers and he was going to do vegetables?"

"Right, but he really wants these roses. So he can mess with them, not me." I sighed. "Except I have this feeling I'll end up taking care of them. I'm becoming mistress of the front yard. Actually, this gardening stuff is kind of fun. Sort of."

Therese smothered an "I told you so" grin. "Just make sure they get lots of sun and lots of air and they'll be fine," she said. "Keep an eye out for black spots on the leaves, and white fuzz. And check them every so often for aphids."

"Aphids? What in God's name are aphids?"

"Tiny, little pod-shaped bugs. Really tiny. Really gross. Bright green. They suck the moisture right out of plants, like little buggy vampires. And they love roses."

"Great." I took another sip of my mocha. "What do I do for them?

And who's going to tell me this stuff when you're gone?"

"I'll be here until August. It's not even May yet. And there's always the telephone." Therese smiled.

I sighed again. Therese was moving to Berkeley to begin graduate studies in theology. I would miss her. "You'll miss Starbucks."

She smiled again. "There's always Peets."

"True, true." Peets Coffee is nearly as widespread in Berkeley as Starbucks is in Portland. Whatever else happened to her at graduate school, Therese would not be suffering from gourmet caffeine withdrawal.

"So go home when we're done here and dig some nice big holes, one for each plant." Therese was back on the roses. "Dig in lots of stuff. Anything, actually. Manure, peat moss, whatever. Then just let it sit in a big mound until the roses arrive. That gives the stuff time to seep into the soil, gives the plants a better start than if you just dig the hole when they arrive. Of course," she gave me a look from under her thick black eyebrows, "it would have been better if you'd dug the holes in, say, February or March and given the stuff a really long time to soak in."

"In February or March I didn't even know I was going to be stuck with roses," I pointed out indignantly.

"You'll need a good pair of pruning shears, as well," Therese continued, ignoring me. "If you prune with an old, dull pair, you'll mangle the branches and then all sorts of nasty bugs and diseases move in."

"Prune? I have to prune them? How on earth do I do that? And when?"

"Not for a while. And just check any gardening book for the how-to. It's easy. You know what?" Therese took a sip of coffee, and I braced myself. "You should start reading the gardening column in the newspaper. They run a little checklist about when to do what. It helps keep me on track every year."

"Hmmmphh," I said, remembering the gardening column of long ago that had suggested pulling weeds during the long, beautiful summer evenings. I did not think that this was the sort of guidance I wanted.

Later that afternoon, Kevin helped me dig the rosebush holes. While we were at it, we dug holes for each of the rhododendrons as well. Then I broke open the box of rhododendron food and, following the instructions, scratched a handful in lightly around the root zone of each azalea and watered them well.

A week later, a truck bristling with plants pulled up in front of the house. Kevin helped the two guys unload the fruit trees, rosebushes, and rhodies, and I directed their placement: roses against the west fence, rhodies up against the house, facing south. The daphne and lilac had already been planted at the far west side of the house, also facing south.

"Nice azaleas," one of the nursery guys said, gesturing toward the pink blossoms.

"They are, aren't they?" I smiled. "Best thing about the yard, so far."

I examined the tags on each rose: Angel Face, a soft purply pink; Apricot Nectar, a pretty peach color; Jeanne Marie, a tall, stately . . . hey, wait a minute!

"Jeanne Marie?" I said to Kevin in disbelief. "You bought a rose named after my oldest sister?"

"I didn't know that was her full name," he protested.

I quickly scanned the rest of the tags, half expecting to see

Elizabeth Anne and Mary Therese. Maybe even Jeanne Marienne, in honor of my mother. Nope, just Precious Platinum, Red Devil, and Chrysler Imperial. Great. A big ugly plant named after a big ugly car. I sighed and watched the truck roll away. It was probably too late to send the roses back.

"You're sure they're going to be okay on this side of the yard?" Kevin asked as we planted the first rose.

"Yes," I said shortly, pulling a thorn out of my gardening glove. As it turned out, I was wrong. Those roses were most definitely not okay. In spite of my confident predictions, they didn't get enough sun. That, combined with Portland's trademark heavy clay soil, which needed far more work than we'd put into it, brought on a whole host of problems—rust, black spot, an aphid infestation of biblical proportions, some sort of fuzzy affliction, and, just as I'd suspected, my own gradual assumption of the rose care. If I'd known what was in store for those roses, I'd have snuck outside that very night and torched them.

The roses had one big thing in their favor: Slugs didn't bother them. By the time late May rolled around, I was, by necessity, a real pro at slug tossing. The neighbors looked on with mild interest. Connie and Mary said actually touching slugs on a regular basis was a little more than they were up for, but that I was welcome to come toss their slugs any time I liked. Bruce, who was looking thinner every day, told me I was just plain crazy. I didn't care. It worked, and it gave me a good upper-body workout four mornings a week after my run in Laurelhurst Park.

Mom and Dad were thrilled with my newfound interest in gardening and on my thirty-second birthday presented me with Ann Lovejoy's book *The Year in Bloom*. I immediately opened the book to the index entry for slugs. There were ten listings, of which "Slug boots" sounded the most promising. I turned rapidly to that page.

Ms. Lovejoy, an avowed nonviolent type, advocated stomping on slugs with heavy garden clogs. I'd already considered and rejected the idea of slug stomping, so I kept reading. Beer, metaldehyde, yeah, yeah, yeah. Then, there it was: Slug tossing! Yes! Someone else was slug tossing! It was comforting to know I wasn't the only one who threw the slimy little creeps into the street.

My slug tossing continued into the early summer. Alder Street didn't get much traffic, but I earned a few glares from motorists whose windshields nearly collided with the early-morning airborne slug delivery. Most mornings I found enough slugs to keep me tossing for at least ten minutes. I learned the joys of watching two, three, four, as many as seven slugs go sailing into the street with a single throw. Maybe this was the same thrill that kept that English malacologist out in the garden night after night. Maybe it was just a new habit taking hold. For whatever reason, what I had dreaded as a time-consuming, boring task became an enjoyable morning ritual. Slug tossing gave me the chance to inspect and enjoy the flowers while also having the satisfaction of knowing that I was ridding them of all visible slugs.

"Visible" is the key word here. The fact that I had to slug toss four mornings a week says something about the reproductive prowess of the slug. A six-year life span (for some slugs) and five hundred eggs per season mean three thousand potential offspring. And those eggs grow up fast. A few months after hatching, it's hard to tell mama slug from the recent infant. And then those babies start having babies.

Once in a while, when I tossed pairs of closely intertwined slugs, I was reminded where all those babies come from. I tried to convince myself that they were just slugs, after all, not capable of great passion or attachment.

Slugs are serious about their egg-producing duties; their mating rituals make most human sexual encounters look boring. Great gray garden slugs occasionally copulate while hanging head down from threads of springy slime. And banana slugs go through a courtship dance that can last for hours. With both banana slugs possessing both sets of reproductive organs (and with male organs sometimes half the length of the slug body), things can get a bit complicated. Banana slugs sometimes become so closely entwined that, in order to separate and get on with life, the female-acting slug uses its teeth on the male to put a sharp and decisive end to the tender moment.

It's dangerous to study too closely any critters that you want to get rid of. The more you know, the harder it is to overlook their good points and kill them simply because they're a nuisance.

"You know what? Slugs are the perfect pet for today's kids," I told Kevin one morning as I came in the front door.

"How so?" He looked up from a bowl of cereal and the sports page.

"Well, think about it. They don't need to be walked. They're pretty portable. They'll eat just about anything from the garden, so they don't need special pet food. And they're supposed to be sluggish, so you don't have to buy little slug exercise wheels. This could be the next big fad. You could even put two in a cage and have slug babies after a while. Truly educational."

Kevin was silent for a minute, then he said, "Meg, I think you're spending too much time in the garden."

Compared to a serious Portland gardener, I wasn't spending nearly enough time in the garden. The front beds still consisted of heavy clay soil with long stretches of dirt interrupted by stiff, awkward groupings of wilting bulbs and relatively perky pansies and petunias. Weeds sprouted and flourished more quickly than I made time to rip them out. And some of the wildflowers that the former owners had planted in the wide front garden bed began to come back. I couldn't tell what was weed and what was flower, so I refrained from pulling anything at all. The result was a big green mess.

At first, the roses did okay without much help. As I had predicted to Therese, I ended up doing most of the rose care—after all, I was right there in the front yard taking care of the rest of the flowers. What were six more plants? I watered them, and pulled a few weeds, and watched the buds develop. I even read a few articles about rose care. But I drew the line at spraying. I wasn't sure what to spray for— mildew? bugs? mold?—but the thought brought to mind clouds of noxious chemicals drifting in dark green, nasty-smelling puffs across the yard. "You simply can't have great roses without spraying them," said one article. Fine, I thought. I won't have great roses.

In late June, I made another trip to Portland Nursery. I was looking for plants that would help fill in the bare dirt: more pansies, some begonias, lobelia, cosmos, snapdragons, stock—all things that *Basic* recommended as good filler plants. This would not be a repeat of last fall's bulb-buying frenzy, I told myself sternly as I drove toward the nursery. This would be a serious approach to coordinating colors and textures. I had to treat this just as if I were decorating the living room.

The fact that our living room (still flaunting that horrid peach color on its walls) consisted of a nine-year-old futon covered in worn gray cotton chintz, a floral couch, a formal Chinese rug that complemented neither the futon nor the couch, two old brass lamps liberated from my parents, and an ancient coffee table I'd inherited from my grandmother didn't stop me from thinking I could coordinate our garden.

My resolve lasted until I got to the nursery and smelled the sweet alyssum. This flower wasn't on my list—I'd never even heard of it— but the short green plants with flowers in hues of white, pink, dark purple, and sky blue had such an intensely sweet fragrance I knew I had to have lots of them. I crammed eight containers of 'Carpet of Snow', a pink 'Rosie O'Day', and three containers of deep purple 'Oriental Nights' into the little red wagon. Each container held at least twenty separate plants. I added deep purple, bright yellow, and shocking orange pansies ("Aren't their faces just like little kittens?" my mother's voice rang in my head), intense blue lobelia, pink and yellow snapdragons, and, as a last-minute splurge for the cats, three catnip plants. "I am crazy," I muttered as I placed the plants in the back of The Fleshy One.

Several hours and an aching back later, I had progressed from questioning my sanity to making vows of self-imposed nursery exile. I had planted what seemed like acres of alyssum and still had one container to go. The dirt beneath the roses was covered with tiny white flowers and sharp green leaves. Pink and white and purple alyssum surrounded the leaves of the fading bulbs in the front garden bed. The rhododendrons, the azaleas, the lilac all had their share of perky little alyssum planted beneath them. Even the clerodendrum, its spindly trunks supporting a few sullen branches and not more than two dozen sickly green leaves, was graced by several alyssum around its base. The pansies, lobelia, and snapdragons added intense color, but it was the alyssum I noticed when I surveyed my day's work.

The sweet alyssum was more than worth all the aches and pains I endured during my marathon planting session. Sweet alyssum will continue blooming until freezing cold takes it down. I'd planted mounds of alyssum right near the front door; it was the first thing you smelled when you stepped out onto the porch. Some winter days I'd catch a whiff of its fragrance and be amazed all over again that I was living in a city where flowers bloomed year-round and 'Carpet of Snow' was a flower, not a chilly fact of life half the year.

Sweet alyssum is easy to grow and a prolific self-seeder, the perfect flower for anyone who's more interested in bike riding or swinging in a hammock than in crawling around in the dirt during Portland's summer heat. The self-seeding habit makes it perform like a perennial, although technically it's an annual. If you cut it back about a month after it first blooms, the plants will bloom again and stay compact, rather than getting a little too tall and scraggly.

Because sweet alyssum is so dependable and flourishes in just about any soil—even Portland's dreaded clay—it's often included in wildflower mixes. It can quickly fill in those awkward bare spots that crop up in every garden. It works in rock gardens, clay pots, spaces between concrete pavers and stepping stones. It's also good in hanging baskets and window boxes. But don't plant it if you like your plants controlled and predictable. Sweet alyssum will get into places you never planned on. This can be a nice surprise, like the day I got out of the car and noticed several sweet alyssum sprouting up through the cracks of our concrete driveway.

Early one July morning, before the heat got intense, I went outside to begin what was becoming a surprisingly enjoyable morning routine: Toss any slugs I could find. Pull the most obvious weeds. Take several deep breaths of the faint alyssum and rose scent already drifting in the air (mostly compliments of Cecile; the new roses had put out very few blooms). Tour the garden to see how the plants were doing. Appreciate the clear sky and thank the Lord I lived in Portland, where a garden didn't require much time or talent.

As I paused near the rose bushes in the west garden bed, my appreciation of the dawning day turned to horror. A sticky, shiny substance coated all six of the plants. Flowers hung limply from their stems. Unopened buds had been munched through. Masses of tiny, bright green, pod-shaped things clustered on each branch of each rosebush. I tentatively prodded some of the green things, and they squished beneath my fingers. Then I stood still for a long time, saying very bad words under my breath.

I would need to make a phone call to Therese to be sure, but it looked like we had aphids.

Therese hadn't been fooling when she'd described aphids as gross. Aphids are even more disgusting than slugs. And in addition to being unredeemably repulsive, the sticky honeydew that aphids excrete after sucking the life out of your flowers makes plants susceptible to flies and ants and sooty mold. I would have no philosphical problem with killing aphids.

Abolishing aphids requires either intensive, ongoing hands-on control or massive amounts of chemicals. Neither option is particularly appealing, but there are low-tech things to try before resorting to the heavy artillery.

On the low-tech end, aphids can be removed by hand and either squished dead between your fingers (ick! ick!) or drowned in a bucket of soapy water.

Another option is the plain water spray. A strong stream of water from the garden hose will knock most aphids off plants. The trick here is to make the water stream hard enough to do the job, but not so strong that it shreds the blossoms. This takes some practice, as I found out to my roses' dismay.

After a few days of patrolling for and killing aphids, it was clearly time to move up the weapons scale. I headed for Portland Nursery and bought a bag of ladybugs, which I'd heard could do great things for insect control.

Supposedly, if you release a bunch of ladybugs, they'll settle down on your plants and eat every aphid in sight. It didn't exactly work that way in our garden. I released the ladybugs, who took one look around and promptly flew over the fence into Mary's yard.

Trying to convince ladybugs to come back home would probably be as successful as herding cats. I stared at the escapees for a few moments, got into The Fleshy One, and roared back to Portland Nursery. Short of ripping the roses out (not a bad idea, really) or bombarding them with heavy chemicals (a really bad idea), I had one final option: insecticidal soap.

Soap sounds pretty safe, but the insecticidal soap bottles at the nursery were loaded with warnings: Keep away from unprotected skin. Do not inhale. Wash hands thoroughly after using. Do not spray in your eyes. I snorted, remembering a label I'd seen on those pressed-wood logs you can buy for your fireplace: "Caution: Fire Hazard." Well, I should certainly *hope* so.

On the way out, I stopped at the nursery's tool display. I would need pruning shears to help me deal with the ravaged roses. Dozens of bright, gleaming tools hung on a wall near the checkout counter, kind of the way candy bars are stocked in a grocery store. *Tools as impulse purchase*, I thought. *What a marketing concept.*

And speaking of marketing concepts, what *were* all these things? Hedge shears, grass shears, houseplant shears, floral shears, floral snips, saws, folding saws, loppers, extenders, rose thorn removers, a two-pocket hand tool carrier that closely resembled a gun holster. All I needed was a pair of plain old pruning shears, the size that fits in your hand. But even plain old pruning shears came in about a dozen different options. I stared, baffled. How on earth would I decide?

Finally, I made a swoop for a pair with cute, fat, red rubber handles and short, sharp-looking blades. The color reminded me of Roxanne, a small, bright red car I had owned a few years before. These shears were described as all-purpose, but it was the red handles that sealed the deal. That, and the fact that they were one of the few options under thirty dollars.

Back at home, the new red pruners made short work of the wilted, aphid-covered rose stems. Then I mixed the insecticidal soap with water in a spray bottle and attacked the aphids still left on the other rose stems. Soap is a contact insecticide (you have to actually put the product right on the bug), and I filled the spray bottle twice before I was done.

It was labor intensive but effective. Aphids shriveled right before my eyes. Entire sheets of green, writhing insect bodies slid off the roses and into a heap on the ground. Wincing, I scooped up their remains, put them in a small plastic bag, and tossed it in the garbage.

Any disease or condition that attacks a plant makes it more susceptible to other predators. As I worked, I saw suspicious black spots on some of the leaves. "God give me strength," I muttered. By the time I was done stripping off all the diseased leaves, our roses looked like a gardener with a grudge had been turned loose on them.

Which, come to think of it, wasn't too far from the truth.

By the next day, the roses looked even worse, limp and naked in the July heat. Resisting the impulse to rip them out by their roots, I instead pointed The Fleshy One toward the International Rose Test Garden in Portland's West Hills. Seeing a few acres of gorgeous roses in full bloom might give me a little more enthusiasm for the scraggly bushes in my own yard. I might even see a city-employed gardener working in the beds and pick up a few tips about rose care.

On a hot, sunny July day, the Rose Test Garden can get pretty crowded. Three tour buses were in the parking lot when I arrived, and a fourth pulled up as I got out of the car. Some of the tour takers headed for the Japanese Garden located across the road, and the others walked down a flight of brick steps into the Rose Garden, joining a crowd of moms with babies in strollers, hand-holding couples bent on romance, and tourist types with cameras slung around their necks. The mingled scent of thousands of rose blossoms hung heavy in the hot air.

I fell in step behind one rather fearsome older woman and her two companions.

"Black spot," she said, pointing to a nearby bush. Her steely tone of voice left no doubt that black spot would never have the nerve to appear in her yard. I half expected her to brandish a cane and take a whack at the offending plant. "They must be falling behind on their spraying schedule. My roses are sprayed with triforine regularly from spring through the end of summer, and I never have a problem with black spot. Or aphids. The malathion takes care of *them*. I wonder if they're feeding these plants properly. They look like they could use a good strong dose of rose food. *My* plants are fed every two weeks, like clockwork." She looked around, probably trying to spot a city gardener to harangue.

"Umm-hmmm," said one of the other women, who had obviously heard it all before.

I wandered away from Mrs. Malathion and into the Shakespeare

Garden, which was filled with old-fashioned flowers. A plaque near a stone-etched portrait of the playwright read, "Of all flowres methinks a rose is best."

Sorry, Will, but I can't agree. Maybe the flowers, or rather, *flowres*, in his day took less work.

"How are the new rose bushes?" It was two weeks later, and Bruce stood on his front porch, smoking a cigarette and watching his dog, Hoffmann, and Connie's cat threaten each other. *La Bohème* poured out of Bruce's open front door into the quiet Southeast Portland morning. "Cosmos, *no*. Hoffmann, come here." He threw the cigarette butt, still smoldering, onto his front walk.

"Hate 'em." I marched grimly down the driveway with my arms full of yet another load of black-spotted leaves. "Black spot, aphids, some creeping crud I can't tell what it is. Hate 'em."

"That's funny. Nothing like that ever happens to my rosebush." He pointed to a full, flowering pink shrub just beyond his front porch. "And it blooms like crazy all summer long."

"Probably been there forever, just like Cecile," I said, gesturing toward our pale pink bush and dropping a few diseased leaves onto the driveway. "I think these new roses aren't as tough or something." I watched Hoffmann transfer his attentions from Cosmos to Pug, who was sitting serenely on our front porch's bottom step. "Hoffmann," I said sternly.

"I'll bet yours aren't getting enough sun," he said. "They probably need a southern exposure, like mine. Hoffmann, *come here.*"

Great. Now my next-door neighbor who mowed his grass once every six weeks and probably hadn't planted a flower in his entire life was a garden expert. I glared at Bruce and snapped, "They get plenty of sun. Hoffmann, *no.*" Pug had retreated up the porch steps, hissing, his tail fluffed out and his ears laid back. Hoffmann turned away reluctantly and trotted back across the driveway to Bruce.

"Well, whatever. By the way, I'm getting a roommate. Someone to help with the rent. I warned him about the Neanderthals around the corner, but he didn't mind. Said he didn't think they'd bother him."

"They haven't bothered you for a long time, have they?"

Bruce shook his head. "Who knows what sets them off. I can't figure it out."

"So when's this guy moving in? What's his name? Do I need to bring cookies and be neighborly?"

Bruce waved a fresh cigarette in the air. "I think this Saturday, but he's a little young and crazy. It might not be until next week. Don't worry about the cookies."

"Okay." I glanced at Pug, who was still on top of the porch with his fur sticking out in all directions. "Young and crazy, huh? How's it gonna be living with young and crazy?"

Bruce shrugged. "I need the money. Come on, Hoffmann."

They went inside, the broken screen door slamming behind them.

I dropped the bundle of rose clippings and walked over to the porch to stroke Pug. "It's okay, old guy," I told him. "It's okay." I looked over at the roses and muttered, "It had damn well better be okay."

Chapter 8

The Joy of Compost

I spent more time than I wanted that first summer patrolling for aphids and ripping spotted leaves off the roses, my negative feelings growing as rapidly as our bill for insecticidal soap. Maybe Kevin had been right all along—maybe *Bruce* was right, for God's sake—and the roses should have been planted against the house's south-facing foundation. I could ask Therese, but she'd probably agree with the guys, and then she'd bug me about moving them, offering free advice and books on transplanting. Better to feign ignorance. With any luck, the roses would get so diseased we'd have no choice but to rip them out. It was a cheery thought.

Bruce had been right about one thing—his new roommate was definitely young and crazy. The first time I met Sam, I had a hard time talking to his face and not his chest. This was not just because his chest, which was without benefit of a shirt, was so finely chiseled, although that was indeed a distraction. Mostly I had trouble looking Sam in the eye because I was looking instead at his nipple ring. Ninety seconds into our first conversation, I was feeling like a middle-aged, middle-class, Midwestern hausfrau. "Doesn't that hurt?" I wanted to ask. "Can I pull on it? Why in God's name did you have that done? Does your mother know about this?" I kept my curiosity in check, just barely, and Sam and I developed a cordial-enough, waving-hello type of relationship.

When Sam moved in, the music spilling out of Bruce's broken screen door changed from opera to hard rock, and a parade of interesting-looking young men streamed in and out of the house. I had the feeling that Bruce and Sam would not be throwing the sort of parties that Bruce and Ed had thrown. I also had the feeling that we would not be invited to these parties.

Fortunately, the rest of the garden was much better behaved than either the roses or the new neighbor. As the summer progressed, last year's wildflower repeats grew into California poppies and bachelor buttons and three-foot-high cosmos and tiny things that looked like miniature snapdragons. And weeds, which I studiously ignored. After all, they might turn out to be flowers if I just let them grow long enough. In the other garden beds, the sweet alyssum outfragranced every plant in the yard, while the pansies and other plants brightened things up. A batch of orange daylilies, contributed by Mom and Dad, were rapidly taking over a previously bare, totally ignored garden bed that ran the length of the driveway. Even my little patch of grass in the middle of the lawn was doing well, bright green and cheerful, with nary a dandelion to mar its perfection.

Only the clerodendrum sulked. Kevin shot the tree evil looks and muttered about wasting a good spot on a bad plant. I fed it gentle little slurps of liquid fertilizer and spoke to it in soft tones. Apparently, Kevin's karma was much stronger than mine. The darn thing resisted all my encouragement.

Every few weeks during the summer, Keith, the lawn-mowing guy, tackled our lawn. I liked Keith. I wasn't so wild about his big, noisy, power mower.

"Hey, remember when we moved in we said we'd talk about buying a mower?" I asked Kevin one day after Keith had been over. "So how 'bout it? A nice little push mower?"

"Why? Keith does a great job." Kevin looked genuinely puzzled. "And, anyway, if we got a mower, I'd want a power mower. Push mowers are too much work."

"But push mowers are better for the environment," I urged. "And we'd save money. A fifty-dollar mower would pay for itself pretty quickly." I paused again. "Plus, we're homeowners. It just seems like we should own a lawn mower. It's a pretty basic tool." I paused again. "Please?"

Kevin sighed. "Listen, if you really want a mower, we'll get one. But I don't want to be stuck with mowing the lawn."

"Don't worry. I'll help," I said, smiling broadly. "I grew up mowing our lawn and it was about nine times this big. This'll be a piece of cake."

Later that week, I stared in disbelief as Kevin lifted an ancient-looking mower from the trunk of The Fleshy One.

"A used mower?" I asked.

Kevin didn't answer.

I tried again. "I guess I was thinking we'd get a new one," I said. "This thing looks kind of—old."

He dropped the lawn-care relic onto the driveway and wheeled it onto the thick sod of the backyard. "It's in decent shape," he said. "I got it for ten bucks at a garage sale, and I stopped off at that knife repair place on Belmont to have the blades sharpened and the wheels greased. It should be just fine." He grimaced and twisted his head from side to side. Crack. Crack.

"Kevin."

"Sorry." He smiled.

I glared at him, then grabbed the mower handle and pushed on it. The mower stayed put. I pushed again. "Kevin, this thing must weigh a hundred pounds. I can't get it to move."

"Maybe the grass is a little wet. That always makes it harder to mow."

"I don't think it's the grass that's the problem here." I hauled the mower backward onto the driveway and dragged it toward the front yard, a suspicious thought dawning in my mind. Had my loving husband purposely bought an old, heavy, hard-to-maneuver mower? *I'll show him*, I thought, and pushed harder. The wheels turned. Little pieces of grass flew in the air. Twenty minutes later, I'd finished the front yard and was ready for a massage.

"That mower is a piece," I said while I ran a glass of cold water in the kitchen and dumped in four ice cubes. "I bet with a good one, I could do the whole lawn in thirty minutes." I saw him bristle at the implied insult: He'd brought home a defective tool.

"The mower's fine," he said hotly. "I told you cutting the grass was hard work."

"Not if we had a good mower, it wouldn't be," I snapped.

We glared at each other. This is ridiculous, I thought. Here we are, ready to have a major argument over a stupid lawn mower.

"Kevin," I said.

"Meg," he said at the same time.

We both stopped.

"You first."

"No, you."

"Okay. The mower will probably be just fine. I guess I haven't mowed a lawn for a while."

"I was just going to say we can get a brand-new one if you really want it," he responded.

We were both silent for a moment. "Let me try again," I finally said. "It probably won't be too bad."

During the height of summer, the real garden action was in the back-yard, where Kevin's fruits and veggies were going gangbusters. He'd planted corn and tomatoes and peppers, and both early-bearing and ever-bearing strawberries. We had picked our first berry in late May and hoped for a steady crop through September. The fruit trees were the only nonproducers; Kevin had pulled off the fruit buds so that the trees could concentrate on making strong root systems during their first year in our garden.

Other than my ongoing war on slugs, aphids, and black spot, July and August were relatively low key in terms of garden work. I pulled weeds whenever the mood struck, which wasn't often, and watered every third day, or every day when it got really hot. Most of our free time was spent on our bikes, or swinging in the hammock, or hanging out at Rooster Rock, a beach in the Columbia River Gorge.

We also visited a local farmer's market held every Saturday morning near the Broadway Bridge in downtown Portland. We brought home a lot of organically grown produce; we threw away a lot of organically grown produce scraps. The wastebasket under the sink began to emit a faint but disgusting odor. By late July, whenever I opened the sink cabinet, the smell of wet, old, rotting produce was unpleasantly noticeable.

"That does it," I said after one particularly noxious encounter. "I've waited nearly a year, and I'm not waiting any longer. When I go to Freddy's today, I'm buying a garbage disposal."

Kevin shook his head. "No, don't. I want a compost heap," he announced.

I stared at him. "A compost heap? Why in God's name do you want a compost heap?"

"Why not? *You're* the one who wanted a push mower. *You're* the one who won't use chemicals on the lawn. A compost heap is about as natural as it gets."

I wrinkled my forehead, stunned but trying to marshal some facts in favor of garbage disposals. "Yeah, but a garbage disposal is just part of modern life. We've had one in all our apartments, remember? And my parents tried a compost heap, and it never really worked. Just lots of rats and possums and raccoons showed up." I was gathering steam. "You don't want rodents around, do you? They'd beat up the cats. Or give them rabies or something. And it would smell. And the neighbors would hate us. It just seems unsanitary."

"Oh, it is not. It'll be great. Trust me."

That day at the store, I looked wistfully at the garbage disposals and their promises of quick, easy cleanup. "One-Touch Operation!" "Easy Installation!" "No More Messy, Smelly Food Scraps!" I sighed and pushed the shopping cart away from temptation.

When Keith mowed the lawn several days later, he left the grass clippings piled in the corner of the backyard. "Kevin asked me to," he explained, when I questioned the green heap. That next weekend, Kevin went to Portland Nursery and came home with a compost bin, a small box labeled "Compost Starter," and several pamphlets printed on dull gray recycled paper. Staring down at their titles—"Compost and You: The Natural Cycle," "The Art of Composting," and "A Sense of Humus"—I knew my garbage disposal was doomed. I filled the teakettle, turned on the stove, and waited to hear the worst.

Kevin sat down to study the pamphlets.

"We need a base of dead leaves," he said after a few minutes.

"Guess we can't start until this fall then," I said, perking up.

"No, there's that bunch of leaves up against the back fence that we never got rid of last fall. And remember those cornstalks from Halloween? The ones that sat on the porch until Christmas? They're out near the leaves. We can break them up and use them, too. That will make a good base. Then, let's see." He went back to reading. The water in the teakettle boiled. I poured it into my mug and let the tea strainer bob around for a few minutes. Kevin continued. "Okay. Then every time the grass gets cut, we just add the clippings to the heap. We should have Keith leave them on the lawn so they dry out first. And we bring out the food scraps from the kitchen and bury those in the middle of it all. That keeps the rats and other critters away. You bury the food so they can't smell it." He shot me a dirty look when I muttered, "Yeah, right," then returned to his reading. "And we have to water it every so often. And put on that compost starter I got. Although this says a splash of ammonia will work just as well."

"Ammonia?" I made a face and took a sip of tea. "We'll have every cat in the neighborhood over here."

"Like we don't already," he said, referring to the steady stream of feline visitors to our front porch water bowl.

"Right. Whatever. Sounds like a lot of work, though." I was not so secretly hoping the heap would bomb and I could get a disposal after all.

"No, this will be fun. Think of it as an adventure. Plus we get worms. Lots of happy worms are the sign of a good compost bin."

"Worms?" I said incredulously, but Kevin was already heading out to the backyard to set up the bin. I followed, tea mug in hand, wondering how to sabotage the operation, wondering how I had managed to marry a man who was fascinated by the miracle of nature as presented in a pile of rotting vegetation. This sort of character flaw should have been disclosed before the marriage vows took place. "Umm, Meg, I'd like to marry you but you need to know that at some point in my life I will be overwhelmed with the urge to heap raw food scraps in our backyard."

The compost bin was a simple, four-sided thing of heavy, plastic-coated wire mesh that stood about three feet high and was about three feet long on each side. Kevin decided to put it in the northwest corner of the yard, well away from the back door and the bedroom windows. "So it won't be the first thing you see when you look outside," he explained.

"Or the first thing you smell," I said.

He ignored me. Using a shovel, he roughed up the dirt where the heap would sit. "That's to give it some breathing room," he said.

"Right." I felt a sudden desperate need for an iced mocha and a really huge, really gooey chocolate chip cookie. A big piece of dark chocolate wouldn't hurt, either. Anything to take my mind off this intentional creation of a pile of smelly, rat-attracting garbage.

I watched as Kevin set up the bin and then walked over to the back fence and began picking up armfuls of dry leaves.

"It would work better if these leaves were chopped into small pieces, because that gives the bacteria more surface to chew on, so things decompose faster. But I guess we'll have to just use them like this. Too bad Keith's not around. We could have him run the leaves over with his mower. Maybe we could just sort of shred them by hand. Nah, too much work."

I considered my husband looking wistfully at a pile of dead leaves. He was awfully cute when he got engrossed in a problem.

"Look, just tell me that it's not going to smell and attract small animals with beady eyes and nasty diseases, okay?"

"It won't. I promise. Okay, here we go. First the cornstalks, then the leaves, then some grass clippings, then some more leaves, then some of the compost starter. Then we just add food scraps when we have them. Wanna give me a hand here?"

I could tell the truth, or I could avoid starting a fight. *For better or for worse*, I reminded myself. If this was as bad as it got, we'd do okay. I put my tea mug down on the porch railing and picked up a load of dry leaves.

Thirty minutes later, I sipped my now-cool tea and watched as Kevin lightly watered the completed heap. "Why is a garbage disposal too much to ask?" I asked, knowing it was too late but unable to stop myself. "It would be so *easy*. I don't want to be carrying food scraps out here in the rain all winter long."

"Don't worry. I'll take care of it," he assured me.

I thought about the roses. I kept my mouth shut.

If we were going to intentionally introduce rotting vegetation into our backyard, I wanted to know something about how this particular act of nature worked. After helping Kevin build the initial heap, I sat down with his composting pamphlets, *Basic*, and *The Year in Bloom*.

The pamphlets reminded me of how crazy I felt when I was first learning about digging amendments into the garden beds. Carbon. Nitrogen. Acid. Alkaline. Ammonia. Aaagggh! *Show me the real stuff*, I thought, *the stuff about odors and rats and irate neighbors*. I turned to the two books.

The Year in Bloom took a laissez-faire approach: Toss the stuff in a container in a corner. Shred it, don't shred it, toss it, don't toss it, whatever. It will eventually break down whether you mess with it or not. No information from Ms. Lovejoy about smells or ill-tempered visitors with sharp teeth.

Basic delivered two pages packed with information about what to use, and how often to water it, and what sorts of nifty containers to build to put it all in. One of its illustrations showed a three-sectioned composting bin that looked to be approximately the size of The Fleshy One. But there was only one short caution about icky smells, and an equally brief mention of the possibility of "hordes of flies." Flies sounded gross, but not as gross as rodents. Maybe I was worrying too much.

In theory, at least according to everything I read, composting is pretty simple: You try to create an efficient rotting environment. This means balancing dry materials (which are high in carbon), wet or "green" materials (high in nitrogen), water, and oxygen. As bacteria and fungi begin to chew on the raw materials, heat builds up in the center of the heap. The heat accelerates decomposition. Turning the heap moves new material into the center, allows oxygen to circulate, and helps everything break down evenly.

Lots of food scraps are perfect for composting: eggshells, raw vegetable peelings, fruit and fruit rinds, tea bags, coffee filters, big bags of coffee grounds from Starbucks.

According to Kevin's pamphlets, certain things absolutely must not get into the compost: oils of any type and animal products such as meat, dairy, fat, bones. That means no leftover salad with dressing on it, no bread or bread crumbs, no fish. No kitty litter or doggy droppings, either.

"Put trimmings from plants that have been exposed to an herbicide, or lawns that have been chemically treated, or trimmings from plants with diseases such as black spot, rust, or mildew into the trash can," I read. Well. That would leave out most of the rose trimmings.

When I was done with the pamphlets, I sat back and considered my options. Option one: I could sabotage the heap by putting all the wrong things into it and making sure it smelled and attracted neighborhood thugs of the wildlife variety; then I would declare the heap a disastrous, dangerous, malodorous failure, march out to Freddy's, and buy my garbage disposal. Option two: I could follow these admittedly simple rules, keep hundreds of pounds of waste out of the local landfill, enrich our garden, save money, and help make my husband happy.

I sighed. Sometimes being a grownup is just no darn fun.

Four short weeks after the compost heap entered our life, the lawn mower exited. After one particularly trying episode in the August heat, I told Kevin we could sell the damn thing to some unsuspecting patsy and ask Keith to take over again. Without a single "I told you so" or even a knowing glance, he picked up the phone.

The next day, I watched wistfully as Keith moved his smelly, noisy mower around the yard. Maybe I'd ask for a brand-new push mower for Christmas.

"Hey, tell me if you smell anything weird coming from over here," I said to Mary one day as we chatted over the side-yard fence. "Kevin's on a compost-heap kick." I pointed to the pile.

"Really?" She looked at it, interested. "Those guys," she waved toward the fence that ran across the back end of her yard, "have had a huge one for years. I've never noticed a smell coming from theirs."

"Yeah, well, I hope we're as lucky."

Kevin took his role as compost cop seriously, installing a large plastic container just outside the kitchen door on the enclosed back porch. Theoretically, vegetable and fruit scraps were to be placed there, prior to finding a home in the heap.

"Don't throw that away," he would warn as I tried to save a few steps by sneaking potato peelings or orange rinds into the kitchen wastebasket. Then he'd launch into a lecture about landfill capacity and garbage and water bills. He was a man with a mission, and gradually I got the message: This wasn't just a compost heap. This was a commitment.

Eventually, it became second nature to carry the food scraps out to the plastic container and then to the heap. During the summer we added grass clippings (both fresh and sundried) and dead flowers, most of which were victims of a late heat wave that coincided with our two-week vacation in Canada. Kevin splashed on ammonia once a month and watered the heap weekly during the summer's hottest days. Every other week, he stirred up the pile with a special compost-turning gadget and poked at it and mumbled. One day, a few hours after the grass had been mown and the fresh clippings added to the heap, the mumble became a shout. "Hey, come here and feel this. These grass clippings are *hot*! It's really aerobic in there."

"Aerobic?" I looked up from the hammock where I was reading yet another murder mystery. "What, like it's wearing spandex and bouncing up and down?"

"No, Meg, aerobic as in using air. As in decomposing."

"So we're actually going to have real live compost from that thing, huh?"

"I'm assuming so. After all, that's the whole point here."

And all this time I'd thought the whole point was just to keep me from getting a garbage disposal. I turned back to my murder mystery and left Kevin to contemplate his aerobic heap.

According to people who know such things, the ideal heap ratio should be thirty parts carbon (dry) to one part nitrogen (wet). That means lots of dried leaves, or sawdust, or dried-out grass clippings. But don't worry about actually measuring the ratio in your heap; when heaps go bad, you can tell what's wrong simply by using your eyes and nose.

If your heap smells like ammonia, it probably has an overabundance of nitrogen-rich materials. Poke around a bit. If the layers are damp and slimy and matted together, toss them around and layer in something rich in carbon, such as straw, sawdust, well-dried grass clippings, or dry leaves, to help soak up the moisture and get your heap back in balance.

If the heap smells rotten, like Easter eggs that have sat undiscovered for several months, it's too wet. The treatment is the same as that for a heap with too much nitrogen, with one extra step: When you're done adding carbon-rich materials, use something like a tarp to cover the heap and protect it from rainfall. This is especially important during the rainy season (some years, that's November through June in Portland). Just about anything will work as a compost cover. Kevin used my plastic wading pool. I had to fight to get it back the next spring.

Your nose can also help you detect a too-dry heap. If the heap smells musty, it needs either water or wet materials. This is easy to take care of: Just aim your garden hose at the heap and, without saturating it completely, get it good and wet. Then let it sit. After a week, turn the heap thoroughly and check the moisture. It should feel like a wrung-out sponge. Adding more fresh grass clippings or produce scraps on a regular basis will help correct this problem over the long term.

September in Portland is stunning. The skies are clear blue. The angle of the sunlight changes just enough to give each day a definite feel of autumn, of the year winding down. Even the occasional September heat waves feel different from those of midsummer. Nights cool off long enough to make each morning fresh and crisp. Leaves begin to turn color, fall-blooming plants put on a show, I start to think about how many weekend bike rides we can get in before the rains start in earnest.

The compost heap continued its warm, aerobic ways. It didn't emit a single bad smell. I didn't find rodent tracks in the vicinity, either. It looked as if Kevin had been right about how easy the whole process was.

I planted catnip near the compost and one day, in a kitty-drug-induced frenzy, Whoo scaled the sides of the wire-mesh bin and stood atop the heap with a triumphant and slightly crazed expression. She looked around in all directions, scratched at the top layer of dried-out grass clippings, then turned around four times and settled down with her chin on her front paws. From that day on, the top of the heap was her private territory. She lounged there, soaking up warmth and surveying her domain and occasionally pouncing on any cat who was foolhardy enough to roll around in the catnip right under her nose.

One lovely September Saturday, I lay in the hammock reading the newspaper, drinking iced tea, and wondering how much longer I could put off weeding the front garden beds. Late ears of corn were ripening against the garage wall, tomatoes against the back fence. The strawberry patch was still pumping out fruit. In the front yard, Cecile was producing fragrant blooms and putting the new roses to shame, while the annuals were winding down their show. I would need to buy fresh pansies, and dusty miller, and some ornamental kale before long.

I looked up from the paper as Whoo and K-word chased each other through the berry patch. Pug, the old guy, snoozed under the hammock. A warm, fuzzy feeling of contentment settled on me. Then Kevin broke the quiet day with a shout.

"Worms!"

I rolled out of the hammock, startled. Hadn't we handled that nasty little problem last time we'd taken the cats to the vet?

He stood by the compost heap with a huge smile on his face.

"Worms!" he said again. "Happy worms enjoying life! It's working! We're going to have real compost!"

Oh. *That* sort of worms. I walked over and looked at the hole he'd dug into the heap. There were worms, all right, big, fat ones waving their tubey bodies around, trying to wriggle back into their dark home.

"That's great," I said, and beat a hasty retreat back to the hammock. Worms. Damn! My garbage disposal would remain a dream.

Chapter 9

There's a Raccoon in My Kitchen

hat second fall in the little blue house, I worked more soil
amendments into the front garden beds. Although the dirt
wasn't quite as dense as it had been last fall, it was still
a long way from being light, fluffy loam, that Holy Grail of the garden
books. Last year's bulbs, along with the crocuses, daffodils, and irises
I'd purchased this fall, would rot for sure if they sat for long in this
mud prison. The Fleshy One hauled bags of steer manure and chicken
manure and commercial compost (Kevin had used most of our backyard compost on his vegetable beds) and peat moss. I dumped it all
on the dirt along with bone meal and blood meal, additions suggested
in *The Year in Bloom*.

"What, no lime?" I could hear Therese's voice, even though she was
studying in Berkeley.

"Nope, no limes," I muttered to the dirt. "Go crack a textbook."

The shovel sliced through several of last spring's bulbs. I tossed them onto the sidewalk and kept working.

When I'd finished digging, I replanted the sliced bulbs and added new ones, trying to group them close together for a big splash of spring color. I planted six lily-of-the-valley under the azaleas, then repeated last year's winter flowers in the big front bed: dusty miller, ornamental kale, and pansies, in much larger quantity than last year.

The clerodendrum, which should have been covered with fragrant blooms in late summer and turquoise berries in the fall, had not performed at all. It hadn't even bothered to put out a single bud. Kevin seemed to have forgotten his bad feelings toward the tree; I dug in plant food around its roots and assured it I would take care of it for a second year.

The roses needed one last cleanup before the rains set in, so I stripped off the leaves—too many of them—that were yellowed, or spotted, or shriveled looking. Cecile, of course, was covered with blooms. I cut an armload for the house. The sweet alyssum were still blooming, smelling great and looking like they were ready for anything winter could deliver. I cut a few sprigs to go with Cecile's blooms, even though alyssum drop their tiny blossoms and make a huge mess almost immediately after cutting. Thirty minutes later, with a garbage can lid full of weeds, I decided that my garden work was done for the year.

Wildlife is surprisingly abundant in the city. Our backyard was home to dozens of noisy birds and squirrels, all battling for seeds at the bird feeder, stealing strawberries from Kevin's fruit garden, and taunting our cats. If you included the worms in the compost heap, our backyard was probably more densely populated than downtown's Pioneer Courthouse Square at noon on a sunny weekday.

Animal activity seemed to pick up during our second autumn in the house, probably because we'd left some of the strawberries and tomatoes unpicked. During the day, birds ate corn from a few stunted cobs still hanging on the stalks. The squirrels hung from tree branches and screeched at anything that moved. At night, we spied on raccoons lumbering around the garden.

"Nature. Ya gotta love it," Kevin said more than once as we looked out the kitchen window.

And love it we did, even when I spotted a trail worn through the grass from Bruce's backyard to our compost heap. Pointing out the animal freeway, I halfheartedly lobbied for a garbage disposal ("I was afraid that heap would attract critters"). Kevin was unmoved. The heap stayed. We were more careful than ever to bury our food scraps in the middle of the heap, but the parade of critters continued.

"How much does this bother you?" Kevin asked one morning when I mentioned the trail for the fourth time in a week.

I thought for a moment. "I guess it's not that big a deal. At least the heap doesn't smell. But I do worry about the cats getting attacked by a raccoon or a possum."

"Well, no one's been in a rumble yet. We could," he said casually, "get one of those big black plastic compost bins that has solid sides and a lid. That would keep the animals away."

"That sounds like a good idea," I agreed. Great! Now we'd get rid of the wire-mesh heap and be done with the critters. I should have paid more attention to Kevin's careful tone of voice.

Kevin bought the black plastic bin the next weekend. I pulled fallen maple leaves from the strawberry patch and watched over my shoulder as he assembled the bin. "Shouldn't you put it over there," I said, motioning across the yard at the original compost heap, "so it's easier to shovel the stuff from that heap into the new one?"

"I thought I'd just start a brand-new heap," he said. "After all, we've got all these dead leaves, too many to put in that first heap."

"Rake them into the street for the city leaf pickup. Besides, I thought the whole point of this was to get rid of the critters." My irritation came through in my voice.

"Oh, we'll be okay," he assured me. "Pretty soon, there won't be anything left for them to steal from the first heap, and I'll put all the new food scraps in here. No animal's going to break into this thing." He thumped the sides of the heavy bin. "It'll be great." He grinned at me.

In spite of my irritation, I grinned back at him. He's hard to resist, and he knows it.

The new compost bin seemed to solve our critter problem. After a few weeks, the grass in the path worn to the compost heap sprang back up. When November rolled around, the second compost bin was nearly full of dead maple leaves and veggie scraps and grass clippings. Possum and raccoon sightings became rarer. By the day after Thanksgiving, we hadn't seen a raccoon in two weeks.

"They don't hibernate, do they?" I asked Kevin as I pulled leftovers out of the refrigerator. We'd had ten people for Thanksgiving dinner and an additional eight for dessert, two of whom were under the age of two, and I was still a little stunned. "Raccoons, I mean."

"What made you think of that?"

"I dunno. Food scraps, I guess." I shrugged. "Do they?"

"I don't think so. Does it matter?"

"Just wondering where they're getting their meals, if not from our compost heap." I dumped turkey into a pan and turned on the heat. Stuffing, mashed potatoes, gravy all went into separate pans.

"They'll survive. I thought you didn't want them in our yard."

I shrugged again, stirring the gravy. "Get out the pumpkin pie, will you, and I think there's some whipped cream left. You're right. I don't want raccoons in our yard, but I kind of worry they'll be hungry."

Kevin rolled his eyes. "Meg, they were fine before we moved here and they'll be fine without our compost heap. Remember that one in San Francisco?"

I nodded. We'd had a regular raccoon visitor at our San Francisco flat. Here in Portland, my parents spent several weeks and more money than they wanted to count having an entire family of raccoons live-trapped and moved from their westside Portland garage three times. And my sisters had had a mysterious visitor to their garbage can in ultra-chic, ultra-crowded Northwest Portland.

There was absolutely no reason for me to worry about the raccoons not getting enough to eat.

Especially after I installed a cat door.

Even the most dedicated cat lover will admit to occasional bouts of impatience with a cat's desire to be on the other side of any closed door. Cat experts say it's all part of the cat's need to patrol its territory inside and out. I say those experts should come and open the door a few evenings for *our* cats. They're not patrolling. They just like seeing us jump up and down. One night, standing at the front door with rain dripping down and a cold wind blowing into the front room, a light bulb went on in my head. A cat door! I had been cheated out of my garbage disposal, but I would not be denied a cat door. "We're installing a cat door," I announced.

Kevin, who was on a business trip, didn't answer. I took this as a sign to go ahead.

The next day I headed over to the cats-only store on Hawthorne Boulevard and came home with the BMW of cat doors. You could adjust this door so that cats could go in and out, or just in, or just out. I got a saw from the basement and went to work.

Two hours and one bloody finger later, I had a brand-new cat door installed in the back door and three cats who steadfastly refused to go anywhere near it. They changed their tune when I plied them with strategically placed tuna. Soon, they learned how much fun it was to be in charge. I congratulated myself on my way with tools and looked forward to cozy winter evenings spent lounging on the couch reading murder mysteries and eating cookies while the cats let themselves in and out of the house.

When Kevin came back from his trip, I showed him the door and the cats leaping happily through it. "What's to keep other cats from coming in?" he asked.

"I don't know why they would," I said. "It's not like we have food right by the door. And if it gets to be a problem, we can lock the door so they can't come in." I demonstrated this nifty feature.

"But then our cats can't come in either."

"Yeah, but they can let themselves out. So at least we'd only do half as much door tending. Don't worry. There wouldn't be such a market for these things if every cat in every neighborhood just roamed in and out of the houses with cat doors."

And I was right, at least for the first few months. No other cats came in our house. No fights erupted over the food bowls. No stray toms sprayed our walls.

Then one night I awoke with the sense that I'd just heard an out-of-place sound. I held my breath, wondering if a burglar was roaming around. The sound of a cat munching on dry food came from the kitchen. I relaxed, then tensed again. Wait a minute. There was one cat asleep near my head, one cat asleep near my feet, and one cat—I squinted in the dark—surely that was one cat asleep near Kevin's feet. That made three cats. Plus the one in the kitchen made four. We only *had* three cats. As I eased out of bed and padded softly toward the kitchen, I heard the cat door flap. The intruder had let himself out.

The next night, we locked the cat door when we went to bed. That solved the intruding cat problem for a while. Then I began finding cats in the house during the day. Some of these cats were strays. Others were cats with whom I was well acquainted. One of them, Connie's cat, ate the exact same kind of food at home that we served at our house. Why he needed to eat at our diner was beyond me.

The cats who were obviously homeless were harder for me to kick out. I began keeping a bowl of cat food on the back porch, hoping this would help them survive and keep them out of the house.

As the winter progressed, it became clear that this was at best a flawed solution. The outdoor bowl of cat food attracted more and more strays, some of which decided to see what was on the indoor menu.

It was bad enough that not all the animals using the cat door were ours. It was worse when we discovered that not all the animals using the cat door were cats.

One evening, I walked into the darkened kitchen. I flipped on the light and saw an enormous raccoon face down in the cat-food bowl. I shrieked. He ran for the cat door and frantically squeezed his pudgy way out.

"What's wrong? Are you okay?" Kevin came running into the kitchen.

"Raccoon!" I gasped. "Eating cat food."

"In here?" he said incredulously.

We stared at each other and burst out laughing.

"That does it, Meg," Kevin said when we'd calmed down. "You can keep the door unlocked during the day, but we're locking it at night as soon as we're done with the dinner dishes."

This plan worked for about a week, until we forgot to lock the door one night and I surprised a possum slinking into the kitchen. We immediately decided to lock the cat door permanently. Our cats resumed howling when they wanted to come in, but the parade of hungry animals through our kitchen ceased.

Locking the cat door wasn't enough to keep out the nastiest critter of all: the *homo burglaris urbanis*. Two nights after Christmas, returning from an evening out, I discovered my top dresser drawer pulled askew and my lingerie scattered on the floor.

I'm a little slow on the uptake sometimes. *Those darn cats*, I thought, then, *Hey, wait a minute!*

"Kevin," I yelled, "Cats can't open drawers, can they?"

"What?"

"Come here." My voice took on an hysterical edge. "I think we've been robbed."

Kevin called 911. I put on the teakettle and rummaged around for an emergency cookie. We found the burglar's point of entry—the window in my study—and the exit—our basement door. I cried. Kevin held me and fumed.

"Cameras, jewelry, petty cash. All small stuff they can sell for drug money," the police officer said thirty minutes later as she took notes. "That's why they left your stereo and the TV."

"Do you think it could have been those guys around the corner?" I asked.

She shook her head. "Believe me, we know all about them. They're not smart enough to do something like this."

We sat on the couch after she left and stared at each other. "I want to move," I said. "I mean it this time."

"I know, but where? Where would we be safe? Your parents and your brother John have both been broken into up in the West Hills. And you know you'd hate the suburbs."

"More crap happens on this side of town. I just want to move," I said stubbornly.

"I know," Kevin repeated. We continued to stare at each other. "I'd love to live outside the city, but let's give it a month or so and see how we feel then," he suggested.

I shrugged. "Okay."

Winter finally gave way to spring. Sam moved out, and Bruce, who continued to look thin and pale, got another roommate, this one not quite so young and not quite so friendly. The Neanderthals around the corner remained mostly out of sight, although every so often one of them would ask if he could mow our lawn or take our returnable bottles.

We had an alarm system installed and perused the real estate ads in the Sunday paper. We even went to a few open houses on Portland's westside. But something didn't feel right. As the shock of the burglary wore off, I realized Portland's eastside felt like home to me. As grimy as it was, I would miss our neighborhood. I would miss Laurelhurst Park, and Hawthorne Boulevard, and the funky shops and the murder-mystery bookstore and the within-a-five-minute-walk Starbucks.

Burglary or no burglary, I just couldn't see leaving.

Outside, the clerodendrum languished in our front garden bed, putting out a few dozen sickly leaves. I sprinkled wildflower seed all around it, hoping to cheer it up. The lily-of-the-valley hadn't made it through the winter, so I planted pansies over their grave. I would try them again next year. Tulips and hyacinths and irises and daffodils fought their way up from the mud, which seemed slightly less muddy than it had last spring. They still weren't as closely massed as I wanted, and some of the tulips and daffodils showed signs of being chewed on, but things were looking up. The lilac put out some blooms—not as many as I'd hoped for, but their fragrance was the intoxicating one I remembered from childhood. I tossed slugs, kept a wary eye on the roses, and cheered when the azalea bushes lining the front bank burst into intense pink bloom. People walking by actually stopped and told me how beautiful the azaleas were. And they *were* stunning—an eye-catching, fluffy pink blanket spread thickly across the entire front yard. It looked like a good year for the front garden beds, with minimal effort on my part.

I actually found myself enjoying the time I spent in the garden. Even weed pulling was fun. And I loved looking at the results: beautiful flowers, grown by the family brown thumb. Just let Therese try to find something wrong with my garden on her next visit home. Hah! I'd show her.

Now it was time to tackle the two backyard beds that weren't destined to grow vegetables.

At first glance, the backyard looked good. It was decent-sized for an urban plot, with plenty of room for Kevin's vegetables and berries and fruit trees, a picnic table and hammock, and, of course, the compost heaps, which now contained everything from food scraps to coffee grounds to a withered Easter lily. One-quarter of the yard was shaded by a neighbor's towering maple; the rest was sunny almost all day long.

The sod had come through its second winter green and healthy.

But the backyard needed some help of the flower variety. Two entire beds were bare dirt. And the fences—old, rusted chain link—were beyond ugly. They made the entire yard look bad.

"We can't afford to replace the fences," I said to Elizabeth one day. She'd stopped over for lunch and a sisterly gossip. "But they just trash the whole backyard. Here, have another cookie. I don't want them around the house."

"So why'd you bake them? Okay, one more. Plant some runner beans to cover the fences," Elizabeth said, munching.

"Beans? I don't even like beans," I protested, my mouth full. "Besides, Kevin's doing the vegetables and I don't think beans are in the program."

She rolled her eyes. "No, Meg, runner beans, not green beans. They're decorative. They'll grow like crazy straight up your fence, and they have white blossoms. Then they put out big, fat, purple and black beans." She caught my skeptical look. "Really, just stick them in the ground near the fence and let them go. Trust me, they're foolproof."

Foolproof, huh? The last time I'd listened to a sister who described something as foolproof, I'd ended up with that spindly clerodendrum. I wasn't going to fall into that trap again.

After Elizabeth left, I leafed through my two garden books looking for plants that would cover the fence. Vines were the most obvious choice—jasmine, wisteria, trumpet vine, passion vine. Ivy and morning glory were out—too aggressive. They wouldn't be content to grow up the fence; they'd grow down and take over the garden beds as well. I settled on clematis and honeysuckle, noting smugly that nowhere were runner beans even mentioned as an option for covering a fence.

By now, The Fleshy One could practically find her own way to Portland Nursery. I turned into the nursery's parking lot, grabbed a little red wagon, and went looking for vines. Half an hour later, I had three clematis, one honeysuckle, and, as a "what the heck" purchase, a package of scarlet runner beans. Perhaps a little contest was in order to see which plant best covered my ugly fences quickly and attractively.

Two hours later, after carefully planting all three clematis and the honeysuckle, I was in no mood to spend much time on the scarlet runner seeds. I more or less threw them onto the ground behind the strawberry patch, poured on some liquid fertilizer and water, and made a mental note to look for bean sprouts in about a week. Given the miserable track record of the supposedly foolproof clerodendrum, I wasn't counting on the beans to do much.

Left to its own devices, some varieties of honeysuckle can completely take over a fence, a bank, a plot of ground. This is a good thing if you like pretty, fragrant vines and have an ugly fence to cover. I planted a variety called Hall's honeysuckle. It rapidly turned my fence into a wall of shiny green leaves and sweet-smelling blossoms.

Honeysuckle does best in full sun, but it tolerated the light shade it got in our yard. I took a few minutes each day to tuck the new, twining tendrils around the openings in the chain-link fence. Once established, the plant was healthy, happy, and needed very little attention—just my sort of garden resident.

Clematis requires a bit more work, but it's worth it if you really like vines. Many varieties are more visually spectacular than the honeysuckle and some are every bit as fragrant.

Unlike honeysuckle, which will grow just about anywhere as long as it gets some sun, clematis has a few really specific requirements, the most important of which is that it hates to have its feet wet. In addition, its leaves and flowers should be in the sun, but its roots require a cool, shady place in which to grow. I puzzled about this when I read it on the plant tag—was I supposed to build a little gazebo on top of the roots?—then decided to cover the root zones with sweet alyssum, whose shallow roots wouldn't interfere with the clematis's growth.

The clematis blooms that first season were few, but big and beautiful. The honeysuckle, on the other hand, put out flowers almost immediately and bloomed eagerly all summer long. Its scent permeated the backyard at midday and wafted in our bedroom window at night.

I completely forgot about the beans until Kevin asked, "What's that in back of the strawberries?"

"What's what?" I looked over from where I was fussing with one of the clematis vines. "Oh, Lord, I can't believe it. It's those scarlet runner beans."

"I didn't plant beans."

"No, I did. They'll climb the fence and cover it, just the way these vines do here." I walked over and tucked the bean tendrils into the open links of the fence, feeling slightly guilty that I hadn't given them any attention.

The summer was a hot one, and the plants needed water nearly every day. Kevin's strawberries bloomed and set fruit and turned bright red in the sun. The roses, which I'd been aggressively spraying with insecticidal soap at the first sign of anything vaguely resembling an aphid, responded fairly well, but I still spent more time dancing attendance on them than I wanted. The orange daylilies along the east side of the house burst into bloom, one after another after another. The flowers in the clerodendrum bed—sweet alyssum, pansies, poppies, snapdragons, lobelia—were bright and cheerful. The clerodendrum itself continued to look slightly ill. We puzzled over a patch of cherry tomatoes sprouting in the flower bed under the front eaves of the house. Where had they come from? Bird special delivery, we finally decided, and enjoyed the tiny fruits warm from the late afternoon sun.

The cats had their horticultural interests, as well. K-word slept under the now-spent lilac and Pug slept beneath Cecile. Whoo continued to prefer the compost heap, where she could survey the yard, guard the catnip patch below her perch, soak up the heap's warmth, and look regal as only cats can. She made an especially striking picture in July, when the composted Easter lily grew straight out the side of the compost heap and produced a huge, white blossom that hovered in the air six inches below her gray and white face.

I swung in the hammock when I should have been pulling weeds and tanned my face when I should have been wearing sunscreen. Kevin messed with the compost, picked strawberries, and talked about building a raised bed for the vegetables that fall. The clerodendrum finally grew a few inches taller and put out a flurry of leaves at the end of the summer that looked almost healthy, although it refused to produce a single blossom. Days were long, evenings were soft and warm. Life was good.

It's at times like these that you get lax about security precautions. We continued using our house alarm, but began unlocking the cat door during the day. One Sunday afternoon, K-word snagged a pigeon and brought it through the cat door into the kitchen, where she let it loose. This was the third time she'd brought in a live bird, but the first time the bird was larger than she. We were torn between telling her what a good kitty she was and ordering her to mend her ways.

Sometimes I'd awaken to the sound of the cat door flapping. I'd count the cats on the bed—usually three—and then go lock the cat door. I didn't mention these incidents to Kevin. I was pretty sure I knew the midnight visitor—a large cat who was mostly Siamese and obviously a stray. Intruder, as I called him, had captured my heart. For some reason, Kevin resisted adopting a fourth feline, so I tried to see that Intruder was well fed, if not well housed.

Like so many well-meaning gestures intended to make the world a better place, this one backfired. On a hot August day, we returned from a five-hour bike ride to discover that someone of the cat persuasion had sprayed all of the downstairs rooms. While Kevin searched for a bucket and some strong soap, I checked the house to see if the perpetrator was still inside. I found Intruder perched on top of the piano in my office, where he'd obviously just finished spraying a picture of three cats that hung on the wall above. I dove at him. He leaped from the piano and sped through the house and out the cat door, nearly knocking Kevin over in the process.

"That does it. We're locking the cat door permanently this time," Kevin said in an "I really mean it" voice.

"It's not fair to restrict our cats because of a neighborhood thug," I protested. "Besides, he just needs a good home and some love."

Kevin glared at me and pushed a wet rag in my direction. "Scrub."

The next day, I called Animal Rescue, a local nonprofit group. A volunteer brought over a live trap, explained how to use it, and gave me her phone number. "Call me the minute he enters the trap," she said. "I'll come get him as soon as I can." She sniffed. "Boy, he did a thorough job, didn't he?"

I blushed. "Yeah, we're still finding some spots."

That night, I put the trap on our back porch, baited it with a big bowl of tuna, and waited. Not more than thirty minutes later, I heard a horrible racket, followed by a cat howling in fright and indignation. Victory! I raced onto the porch to find Pug quivering in the trap. I let him out, hugged him, and offered him all the tuna as a peace offering. He turned up his nose and thumped off, angry, insulted, humiliated.

More than a week and many bowls of tuna later, I finally caught Intruder. He went off with the Animal Rescue volunteer, who would keep him for a few weeks while he was checked out by a vet and adopted into a permanent home. We spent those weeks following our noses to cat-spray spots we'd missed. Kevin grumbled more and made dark remarks about taking all three of our cats to Animal Rescue.

Reluctantly, I agreed with Kevin that the great cat-door experiment was over for good. We locked the door and returned to being butlers for our cats. After recovering from their initial indignation, they learned to bang on the cat door with their front paws when they wanted in or out. Our house was free of pigeons and raccoons and stray cats and stray cat spray, and Nature was back outside where it belonged.

Chapter 10

Poodle Trees Are
Not an Option

I once read an article about dealing with writer's block. The most succinct advice was given by a guy who said he had just one rule: "Butt in chair."

I've tried to adopt this rule. But butt in chair didn't work all that well for me during the last of the long, hot days of summer. It wasn't so much that I had writer's block. I had post-vacation block. We'd just returned from a three-week trip and, on a warm September Monday morning, I was feeling resentful that I had to work. My next deadline was six days away. It could have been six years for all the interest and enthusiasm I felt. A long run in the park followed by a quick weed patrol of the front garden beds did absolutely nothing to propel me into my office.

You need to ease back into this work thing, I told myself. How

about butt on couch? I grabbed a chocolate bar and a book I hadn't
had time to finish on vacation and headed for the unfortunately still-
peach living room. I could always work after lunch.

About an hour into the book, a pickup truck bearing the City of
Portland seal parked in front of our house. As I watched from the
living room windows, a man got out, walked over to our big, beautiful
maple trees, and began poking at them in an official manner. I put my
book down and headed out the door.

"Can I help you?" I called from the front porch.

He glanced up at me. "Your trees are dead. They need to come
down."

"Excuse me?" I sped down the front walk, certain I'd misheard. A
slight twinge of unease twanged at the back of my mind. Maybe I
should have paid more attention to Dad's suggestion, two years ago,
that I call an arborist. But if the trees were dead, why were they covered with leaves? This man was obviously deranged. I'd set him
straight politely but firmly and send him on his way.

He introduced himself as a city forester and flashed an official-
looking name tag. Forester, schmorester, I thought. My clerodendrum
might be just barely breathing, but nobody was going to mess with
my maples.

"They're not dead," I said with all the confidence of the love-blind
ignoramus correcting the expert. "I know that cut in the bark looks
bad, but just look at all those leaves. The trees must be okay."

He tried again. "Really, ma'am, they're dead. There's no way a tree
can survive very long with a cut this deep into its cambium layer."

I hate it when people call me ma'am. Ma'am is what you call dumpy, middle-aged women, and at thirty-three, I considered myself the springiest of spring chickens. "You're not serious."

"I am. Besides this cut, you can see where both the trees were topped at one time." He pointed to huge, ugly lumps high up on the trunks of both trees. The lumps were nearly hidden behind the leaves; even when the trees were bare in the winter, I'd never really noticed the ugly, gnarly swellings. "That's probably when the troubles started. Topping trees weakens them severely." He shook his head, whether in sorrow for the trees or in disgust for idiotic urban tree killers, I couldn't tell. "The leaves are coming from the reserves the trees have stored up over the years. Trust me, you won't want to be around these trees in the next serious ice or wind storm."

"So you really think we should cut them down?" I asked, horrified.

He looked at me as if I were a very slow learner. "Let's just say I hope you have good homeowner's insurance if you decide to leave them up."

We talked for close to half an hour. I relearned everything I'd forgotten from seventh-grade biology class about how trees grow. I found out about replacement trees, which had to be chosen from a city-approved list. I also found out we couldn't leave the parking strip bare even if we wanted.

"So, can we put in this same sort of maple?" I asked, perusing the city's approved-tree list that the forester produced from a folder.

"No, you can't. This type grows up into the power lines. And besides," he said, pointing to the buckled sidewalk, "you can bet you've got roots growing though your sewer lines as well. Maples this big really aren't suited for city life. You can get some of these smaller maples," he gestured at the list, "or any of the other trees listed here."

I scanned the list. Flowering cherries. Flowering plums. No way on either of those: too short, too ugly except for a few weeks in the spring. Hawthorne. Ash. Siberian crab. *Clerodendrum trichotomum*—the harlequin glorybower! Gee, maybe I could talk Kevin into putting one on the parking strip. Yeah, right.

"I want the biggest maple we can put here, and I want it to turn red in the fall," I said.

"The Norway maple might be good. It's about twenty-five feet at full height. That's below your power lines, and the leaves turn maroon."

"Great. So, what happens now? We tell you okay and a city crew comes and takes the trees down?"

"Sorry, ma'am, we don't do that. You have to find a tree-removal service yourself. Then you buy the new trees and either plant them yourself or hire someone to do it."

"What?" I protested, outraged and feeling distinctly un-ma'am-like. "The trees are on the parking strip. The parking strip is city property. The city is telling us we have to take them down. So the city should foot the bill. Besides, I know I've seen city crews taking down street trees and cutting up the branches."

"That's just if a tree has already fallen and is a threat to public safety." He shook his head. "We haven't done street-tree removal for years because of budget cuts. Anyway, decide which trees you want. Call me, and I'll send you a tree planting permit. Then after they're planted, I'll come by to check them out and make sure everything's okay."

"All right, one last thing," I said as he got into his truck. "Can you recommend a tree-removal service?"

He shook his head. "Sorry. We're not allowed to do that. I'd say get three different bids and go with whichever outfit seems the most knowledgeable."

"So, was there any way we could have known these trees were on the way out when we bought the house?" I persisted. "Was it really obvious and we just missed it?"

"It's obvious to someone like me," he said, looking as if he were eager to get on to his next tree condemnation. "Next time you buy a house, call us. The city forester who works in that neighborhood will come by and inspect the trees on the parking strip."

He drove off. I stood stroking the bark of the biggest maple. Then I headed inside to call Kevin with the bad news.

Despite Dad's warning, we'd never really looked critically at our maples. They were just *there*, permanent, solid, seemingly unperturbed by wind or rain. But after the city forester's visit, we learned to recognize the danger signals of unhealthy trees: suckers sprouting from broken limbs, a few branches with leaves that never fully unfolded, other branches that were entirely devoid of leaves, even in high summer.

Urban forestry and basic gardening have several things in common, perhaps the most important being the principle of putting the right plant in the right place. Even I had to admit that, as majestic as they were, those trees were the wrong choice for our narrow parking strip. As the forester had pointed out, roots had buckled the sidewalk. The branches had grown up around the power lines; one large branch was actually leaning on a line. It was a sewer backup and power outage just waiting to happen.

On the other hand, huge maples perform what is sometimes a critical urban function: blocking the sightlines across the street.

"Eee-yuk. Check out what our view will be when those trees come down," I said one evening as we sat on the front porch after dinner and munched fresh chocolate chip cookies. Even during the winter, when the maples were completely bare of leaves, their network of heavy dark branches screened out the view across Alder Street. With the trees gone, we would have an unobstructed view of a small, gray home that resembled a shy, tattered mouse, and a two-story mustard-colored duplex that needed new paint, a new porch, and a new garage.

"Yeah, but it might not be all bad," Kevin said. "Let's look on the bright side. We'll have an awful lot of free firewood. And a couple of flowering plums will look really pretty on the parking strip."

I sputtered into my after-dinner cup of tea. "Flowering plums?" I said in disbelief. "No way. They're the tree equivalent of toy poodles. We're putting real trees there, not yapping little flowering plums."

"You like the way Taylor and Yamhill look in the spring," he pointed out, referring to two nearby streets lined with flowering plums and cherries.

"That's lots and lots of them, ten or twenty blocks worth," I protested. "It's a little different from a lone tree or two. Plus, they have those ugly, dark red leaves. I want green ones. And they're short. I want tall trees."

"The city forester said the trees had to be short anyway," Kevin said.

"Not that short. Please, Kevin. I really, really want maples. They make this house a home."

"You want them because you grew up with them," he said.

"Well, yeah, that's one reason."

"I grew up with flowering plums. They'd make the house feel like home for me."

I had a brainstorm. "How about one of each?"

He thought for a moment, then shook his head. "I think the trees should match."

"Why? I bet we could walk all over this neighborhood and find homes with parking-strip trees that don't match." I put my teacup down and grabbed a cookie for the road. "Let's go."

We walked, and we talked. We saw all of the usual Portland street trees: maples, flowering plums and cherries, ash and hawthorne, a few birch with gracefully peeling bark. Tall rhododendrons did tree duty in a few yards. One parking strip was entirely covered with roses; a dozen bushes marched in a straight line, each bush heavy with blossoms. I was suddenly reminded of my grandmother, who'd grown roses to perfection in her Seattle garden.

"There's an idea," Kevin said.

"Sure, if you'll take care of them," I replied, shaking thoughts of Grandma DesCamp from my head. "I've got enough rose duty on my hands as it is."

"Okay, not such a good idea. I guess we should aim for something low maintenance."

"Yeah, hey, how about *no* maintenance?" I replied.

Kevin laughed. "Sometimes you still sound so Midwestern."

"*Kevin.*"

"No, it's not a bad thing." He smiled.

We stopped at a corner to let a small blue car go by. I was searching for some smart remark to make about West Coast accents when the driver of the car slowed down, leaned out the window, and said, "Umm, can you tell me where I can get some," and then he made the classic puffing-on-a-joint motion.

I burst out laughing, my pique over sounding Midwestern totally forgotten.

"Sorry," Kevin said.

The guy drove off.

"Jeez, do we look like druggies?" I asked Kevin.

"I don't think so. I guess he just thinks this neighborhood . . . you know—" For once, Kevin didn't seem to be able to make a coherent sentence. We walked in silence for a few blocks.

"You know what? The more I think about that, the less funny it is," I said, as we turned onto Alder Street. "I don't want people cruising our neighborhood looking for drugs."

"Hazards of city life, I guess," Kevin said.

"I guess, hey," I said, purposely drawing out the "hey."

We stopped on the sidewalk in front of our house and looked up at the maples.

"Maybe one of each wouldn't be so bad," Kevin said. "I like maples. They're sort of solid looking."

"And I guess a plum wouldn't be totally disgusting," I said. I patted the bark of the biggest maple, and we headed inside for the evening.

"Where did you get this?" Kevin asked, picking up a pamphlet from the kitchen counter.

I shrugged. "The nursery. They had a stack of them, and I thought we'd better know what to do about those trees. I think there's potential for real trouble. The azalea hedge is right underneath some of the biggest branches. What if the hedge gets crushed? That would *ruin* the yard in the spring. Or what if they chop the trees the wrong way and they fall on the house? Or if the cats get hit by a falling limb?"

"Keep the cats in the house. I think you worry too much." Kevin opened the pamphlet and flipped through it.

"How to Hire an Arborist" is published by the National Arbor Day Foundation. It's full of tips on how to tell if you need an arborist, how to select a tree remover, and what to look for in a written agreement. Not surprisingly, the foundation strongly recommends hiring only those who are members of a professional arboriculture association. It also suggests asking for certificates of insurance, written estimates, local references, and proof of certification. The list of cautions is long and strong. "Beware of door-knockers. Avoid arborists who routinely top trees. Don't just phone the arborist's references, drive by and see the work. Never let yourself be rushed by bargains ("I'm in the neighborhood today, so I'll do it for 25 percent off"). Never pay in advance." *As if,* I thought.

Kevin and I talked to tree-removal companies of all shapes and sizes, from the one-person shop with a stump grinder chained in the back of a pickup truck to large outfits with large trucks and even larger advertising budgets.

The large outfits were, not surprisingly, the most expensive. The biggest company we contacted provided a detailed written estimate of the work it would perform and how much it would cost. The representative who came to look at our trees wore a clean, nicely pressed shirt emblazoned with the company's name. "We're pretty busy," he said. "It will be at least four weeks before we can schedule you in. I'll mail you a written estimate, but I'm guessing we could do the full job for about two thousand dollars—cut the trees down, rout out the roots, chip the wood, and haul it away. We do this sort of work all the time, and we'll guarantee your satisfaction."

I gulped. Two thousand dollars was a lot of money, more than we'd paid for The Fleshy One. Add in the cost of buying replacement trees and there went any chance for a week-long tropical escape from the rain next winter.

Small-time operators didn't make me feel any better than the big companies. One guy roared up to the house in a rusty pickup that made more noise than a city bus. He got out, looked at the trees, spit on the sidewalk, and said, "I can do both of them for four hundred fifty dollars, and I can do them tomorrow morning." He peered at me from under a greasy paint-company cap that was jammed low on his head. "Okay?"

"Uh, yeah, okay. I mean, we've just started getting quotes," I lied. "Do you have a business card? I'll call you."

He pulled a grimy card from his back pocket. I tossed it in the recycling bin as soon as he rumbled off.

For more than a week, men poked at our trees and paced around on our sidewalk. After we collected all the bids, we sat down to decide who got the job. The winner was a guy who bid nine hundred dollars. He promised to chop the wood into fireplace-sized logs, grind out the roots, chip the branches, and clean up the sidewalk. He promised to protect the azalea hedge. We called his references, gave him the go-ahead, and braced ourselves for the loss of the maples.

On the September morning of the tree-removal operation, I made an extra-strong cup of tea and stood outside, chatting with Connie about the doomed trees as the guy and his helper donned tree spikes, climbed into the biggest tree, and made the first cuts. Then, deciding it was too painful to watch, I gathered the cats, headed into my office, and got to work. The roar of the machinery was deafening. The crash of branches on the ground was worse. I tried to tune it all out.

After a half hour, I stood up to stretch and took a peek out the window. What I saw made me run for the front door and race out onto the front walk.

I'm never at my most authoritative when I'm intensely angry. My voice goes up an octave and occasionally climbs entirely out of human hearing range. I squeak. I shake. It's hard to make big men with power tools take you seriously when you're behaving like a small, hairless dog.

"Hey!" I tried to make myself heard over the roar of the machines. "Hey! You guys! Stop right now! Just stop!" I was shrieking and waving my hands over my head before they heard me and shut off the power saws.

"The azalea hedge! You were supposed to make sure nothing happened to it!" I started hauling huge maple branches off the hedge. One of the bushes was crushed right down to the ground. Branches on the other bushes were broken and hung limply at unnatural angles.

"Look at this!" I screamed, dragging more branches away and tossing them onto the sidewalk below.

They looked at the branches and then at each other. "Sorry, ma'am. A few branches got away from us," one of the guys said.

Don't you ma'am me. "More than a few," I snapped, finally getting control of my voice. "These azaleas are mangled. You promised to protect them. Stop working right now or else make damn sure nothing else falls on them."

I stood there waiting and shaking. They shrugged again. "We're doing our best," the guy said sullenly. "We'll try to be more careful."

I didn't answer, just headed back into the house. As soon as I closed the door I started sobbing. Bad enough to lose the maples. Losing the showy, healthy azaleas was more than a woman should have to bear. Two years ago I wouldn't have cared. Now, I was outraged.

After a few minutes, I wiped my eyes, blew my nose, and called Kevin at work. His voice mail answered. "Kev. Kevin, it's me," I gulped, fighting back a fresh stream of tears. "Call me, okay? Those tree guys have ruined our azaleas. Shit! Call me."

Minutes ticked by. The machines roared outside. Branches flew threw the air. Every five minutes or so I looked out the windows at the azaleas. They were still there, still mangled. No spontaneous regeneration had taken place, but no more heavy branches had landed on them, either. The parking strip, sidewalk, and lawn filled up with small branches and large tree chips. I waited impatiently for Kevin to call. The phone didn't ring for more than two hours.

"Meg, sorry. I was in a meeting," he said when I picked up the phone. "Are you okay? What's going on?"

"It's awful!" I hollered into the phone. "The azaleas are crushed. The yard's a mess. It all looks horrible. These guys are jerks." I snuffled and blinked back tears. "I hate it when I get like this. It's so ineffective."

He swore under his breath. "Do you want me to come home?"

I wanted to say yes. But I was an adult, wasn't I? I should be able to handle this without falling apart. "No. I'm not sure what you could do now, anyway. They've just about taken out all the big branches. They should be bringing the trees down any time now."

"You call me if anything else goes wrong," he said.

By late in the afternoon, both trees were down and cut into large pieces. The guys got into their truck and drove off without knocking on the door to tell me they were done.

I walked outside to survey the damage. Sawdust and tree chips filled the street, the sidewalk, the lawn, the azalea hedge, the front garden beds. Pansies and sweet alyssum lay crushed under the weight of tree debris. Leaves and small branches were everywhere. The trunks of the trees and the biggest branches had been cut into pieces—large pieces, far too large to fit in the fireplace—and left randomly around the parking strip.

This was their idea of a thorough cleanup job?

I got my cute red pruning shears from the garage and made clean cuts where azalea branches had been crushed or hung broken. "I'm sorry," I said softly as I worked. "I'm so sorry." Then I got the box of rhododendron and azalea food from the garage and scratched it in around the base of each plant, soaking the soil with water. "There, that should help you guys feel better."

That evening before dinner, Kevin and I walked around the front yard while Bruce and his dog, Hoffmann, watched silently from their porch steps. Kevin was furious. I had gone from anger to resigned sadness. Bruce shook his head every few minutes and lit one cigarette after another. With Sam and his loud alterna-rock gone, opera poured out of the broken screen door again.

"I'm calling that guy and telling him we're not paying him. This isn't what we agreed on." Kevin kicked a five-foot-long, foot-thick branch with his foot. "Firewood! This might fit in the fireplace up at Timberline Lodge, but not in ours." He kicked another chunk of wood. "Ow."

"Well, at least we know the trees really were dead," I said, pointing to the stumps, which had been left on the sidewalk. The center of each stump was hollow, with only about four inches of wood remaining inside the outer bark.

Kevin rubbed his kicking foot against the back of his leg. "Yeah, they were dead, all right. I just wish we'd known that when we moved in. Nine hundred bucks would buy a lot of stuff for the house."

"Hey, the joys of being a homeowner." I was actually starting to cheer up, now that things couldn't get any worse. "It's always something. Either your trees are dead or you've got possums in your kitchen."

"Right. Look, I don't have time to clean this up and I don't expect you do either. Let's get someone over here to deal with it."

Keith, our lawn guy, brought his brother and did damage control on the yard, cutting up the remaining big branches and sweeping up the wood chips. Before they arrived, I picked out two huge, hollow pieces of maple trunk and, using Mary's wheelbarrow, rolled them up the driveway. One went into the garden bed at the back of the house, the other in the front bed near the roses.

"What are you doing?" Kevin asked, as I heaped compost and steer manure and dirt into each trunk's center.

"Remembering. Next spring, I'm going to plant flowers in here." I shrugged. "I know I'm a goofball, but I don't want to lose the maples entirely."

"I think it's sweet."

"Yeah, I guess so." I sighed. "I sure will miss those maples."

Chapter 11

Get Your Hands Off My Tree, Buster

G ive me one good reason why we shouldn't dig up this measly excuse for a tree right now," Kevin said, glaring at the clerodendrum wilting in a late September heat wave.

"Okay, here's one. I won't let you," I shot back.

That effectively stopped the conversation for a few moments or, rather, steered it in another direction. But when we got back to arguing about the clerodendrum, the question remained: Should we continue giving space to a plant that had shown minimal growth for two years and looked awkward ("It's just plain *ugly*," Kevin insisted) to boot? Downsizing was the hot topic of the business world that autumn, and Kevin thought we should transfer corporate policy to the home front. To bolster his argument, he pointed out that soon it would be cool and damp—prime time to transplant trees.

"Okay, yeah, so your pear tree needs more sun," I admitted, "but I told you from the beginning I don't want a fruit tree in our front yard. You know what this neighborhood is like. We'll have thugs and bikers coming up on our lawn to steal our fruit. Besides, I shouldn't have to give up my clerodendrum. You've got two trees. I've just got this one." *And I still don't have a garbage disposal or a push mower,* I added silently.

"Why are you so set on keeping this thing, anyway?" he asked. "I thought you hated anything that was a lot of work. You sure gripe about the roses."

I looked at the pathetic, skinny tree and felt a pang at the thought of its potential glory. "I don't know. Because the one Therese grew was so beautiful, I guess. When it blooms, it has the most amazing blossoms and then this shiny, metallic teal fruit. And the smell is enough to make you cry."

He was looking at me with an odd expression.

"No, it's a *good* smell," I explained. "But something about the fragrance makes me weepy, like it's amazing that anything could smell that good. It's how I used to feel about our lilacs when I was a little girl."

"We have a lilac bush," Kevin pointed out. "If you just want to cry, you could go smell that."

I glared at him. "You'll understand what I'm talking about when it blooms."

"*If* it blooms. I think you just want to grow this thing because your sister did. It's that competitive DesCamp thing coming out."

"All the more reason to make the damn tree grow," I snapped.

Even in fertile Portland, it's possible to make a mistake in the garden. It might be a shrub planted in the wrong place or a patch of bulbs standing around with their feet wet. It could be roses struggling in the shade of a large tree instead of soaking up the sun.

Once you've discovered and admitted that you've made a garden mistake (these two events by no means take place at the same time), there are basically two ways to deal with the situation: Rip out the offending plant and start over with something else, or find out what the problem is and correct it, if possible.

The first approach has many advantages: It's quick. It's easy (unless you're removing a huge shrub or tree). When it's over, it's over. You make a clean start and move on.

But if the plant is one you've always dreamed of growing, or can't bear to part with for sentimental reasons, or simply have to grow because of a competitive streak, you can count on spending a fair amount of time finding out what's wrong and how to deal with it.

Short of directly interrogating the plant, the best initial line of inquiry is to talk with someone who's grown it successfully.

"What do you mean, it's not doing well? It's a clerodendrum. It's foolproof!" Therese said over the phone.

That sappy phone-company jingle ran through my mind: *Reach out and touch someone.* I'd reach out and touch her, all right. "Yeah, I know, but it's just not growing. What did you do to yours?"

"Well, let me think." She paused. "I dug in a bunch of stuff first, you know, the standard stuff—"

"Yeah, yeah, compost and manure and peat moss and limes."

"Lime. Singular."

"I'm teasing. I know it's lime singular."

"Right. I probably added some rock phosphate, too, for long-term nitrogen and phosphorus release. You know, instead of bone meal, which is more like an instant fertilizer. Rock phosphate sticks around for a long time and releases nutrients more slowly. Plus it's cheap."

"Cheap is good." I shook my head, a not uncommon occurrence during my talks with Therese. *Rock phosphate. Where did she come up with this stuff?*

"Then, let's see. I just planted it and gave it a fair amount of water that first year and pruned it once or twice and added liquid fertilizer a few times."

"Wait. You pruned it? Why didn't you tell me that earlier?"

"Me-eg." She drew my name out into two annoyed-sounding syllables. "It's just like any other shrubby tree thing, like a lilac or whatever. You have to prune it to give it some oomph and spur its growth."

"I don't prune my lilacs," I said.

"You should."

I moved the phone away from my ear and stared at it. For this I was paying long-distance rates to Berkeley? "Okay, so I'll prune the damn thing."

"Not now. Next year. In the early spring, when it's still dormant. Prune it now and it'll put out new growth that'll just die when the weather turns cold."

Kevin would love that. I made a mental note to hide the pruning shears, said goodbye, and hung up.

Okay, so my personal gardening guru was of next-to-no help. I hauled out *Basic* and *The Year in Bloom*. Neither one of them mentioned clerodendrums. What now? I could call the nursery, that's what.

"Portland Nursery. What can I do for you?"

"I need some info about a clerodendrum that's just not doing well."

"Okay, hold on."

I held. And held. After several minutes, a gentle, soothing voice came on the line.

"Hi. What can I do for you?" He sounded like a person who lived and breathed with the calm, steady rhythm of plants growing in the earth.

I took a deep breath. "I have this clerodendrum, it's a harlequin glorybower and it's just not—it's just not happy. I planted it two years ago and it hasn't done anything."

"Have you fed it anything?" said the soothing voice.

"Yeah, every so often I dump some of that liquid plant fertilizer on it when I water it. You know, that green stuff?"

"Umm-hmmm. I'm wondering if maybe you have a heavy clay soil underneath it?"

I burst out laughing. "Well, yeah, I do."

The voice on the other end laughed gently. "Don't we all. Usually they can take that, but maybe yours has some root rot. I wonder if it might not need some nitrogen and phosphorus. Has it grown at all in height? Or put out more leaves each year than the year before?"

I thought. It *was* a little taller than it had been. And it had a few more leaves than last year: They just didn't look healthy. I said so.

The soothing voice said, "Then what I would suggest is to feed it fairly regularly with a dry fertilizer. Just scratch it in around the drip line—you know, directly below the furthest extension of the leaves?—and water it in really well. But don't do that now. Start in the spring when the leaf buds begin to swell and do it every six weeks or so until about September. That should really help. Usually clerodendrum is one of those plants you can just stick in the soil and leave alone, but yours sounds like it needs a little help."

"It's still pretty short. Do you think I should dig it up and add some stuff to break up the soil?"

"You could do that." The voice took on a mildly cautious tone. "Don't do it until early spring, though. Make sure the plant is totally dormant."

"Okay. Thanks a lot for the help."

"Sure. You know, sometimes plants just need a little time to come into their own."

"Don't we all," I said, and hung up.

While Kevin was busy eyeing my clerodendrum and measuring the front border to see just where the pear tree would fit best, I was mounting an attack of my own.

"I'll make you a deal. You can move the clerodendrum if we can rip out the roses. Hell, I'll rip out the roses barehanded. Nothing would give me more pleasure."

"Rip out the roses?" He looked horrified.

"They're a mess, Kevin, and I'm the one stuck taking care of them while you putz around with your fruit trees and vegetables. For two summers now, I've been constantly spraying them with insecticidal soap to keep the aphids from completely ruining them. They still get black spot. And I'm always going at them with the pruning shears to take off some diseased part. They were a mistake."

"And this wasn't?" He gestured at the spindly tree.

"Yeah, so, it might not look good, but at least it's not eating up my time like your roses are. And the guy at the nursery said . . ."

Roses are the flower of passion, all right. We argued for an entire weekend about the roses, the clerodendrum, the pear tree. I grabbed every garden book in the house (I was up to three by now) and looked for information to back up my point of view. "Look, Kevin, it says here that when you put lots of roses together, they're more susceptible to bugs and crud," I said, waving a book in the air. "And you shouldn't grow new roses where other roses have had problems. It means the soil is bad for roses. They'll never be okay. We should just rip them all out."

"They'd be fine if we put them in that bed in front of the house, the one that faces south," he said. "What do your books say about light exposure? They probably say the roses need more sun than they're getting, right? Tell you what. If we move them, I'd be willing to give your tree-thingy one more year where it is."

"But if we move the roses, we have to move the rhodies to make room for them," I argued. "And what if they *all* die? We're out hundreds of dollars worth of plants."

"How about we just move two of the roses and see how they do? There's enough room to fit them in between the rhodies."

"Hmmm." I thought about this, looking for possible traps. "Okay. I'll help you transplant two of the roses if my clerodendrum can stay where it is. Have you ever transplanted anything?"

"No, but I bet Keith could tell us how."

"Or Therese." I thought for a moment. "Let me check my gardening books before we call anyone."

The books, Therese, and Keith all suggested we wait until late October or early November to move the roses. That gave us plenty of time to dig two holes for them and add lots of dirt food—compost, manure, damp peat moss, even rock phosphate. This easy bit of dirt digging inspired me to take the amendments down to the parking strip and get to work there, where the soil was hard packed and nearly impossible to dig in places. It probably hadn't been touched since the maples were planted ninety years before.

In October, Kevin and I visited Big Trees Today, a tree farm located southwest of Portland. The owner walked us around the property, and we quickly found two plump, healthy trees—a maple and a flowering plum—that were on the city's list of street trees.

"We dig the trees after the rains have set in, usually early to mid-November," the owner said, folding our deposit check and putting it in his pocket. "The ground has to be soft enough to get the trees up without harming the roots. After they're dug, we wrap the root balls up nice and tight for delivery."

"Do you deliver and transplant them?" Kevin asked.

He named a price per tree that made us both blanch. "Or you can do it yourself. Trees this big will weigh at least five hundred pounds each with the root ball." I made a face, and he went on. "It's pretty easy. You don't actually lift the trees. You roll them on their root ball."

I shot a glance at Kevin. This was one time when I was grateful he didn't have the do-it-yourself gene.

"We'll get back to you on that," Kevin said.

"Let's have them do it," I said as we drove through farmland and headed back to Portland. "We know they'll do a good job."

"Well, I'm sure not going to mess around with a half ton of trees. But it's a lot of money." Kevin was silent for a moment. "Maybe Keith can help us."

Keith didn't want the job—something about an old back injury—but he recommended his nephew. The nephew came over to look at the planting sites and we agreed on a price. I crossed my fingers and hoped this wouldn't be the azalea hedge all over again.

The Saturday after Halloween, we dug up the two roses that were destined for transplanting and gently shook the dirt off their roots (roses and other deciduous plants can be transplanted bare root, although most other plants should be moved with their root ball intact). Then we dug all the dirt out of the planting sites we'd prepared, made a little cone of dirt in the middle of each hole, spread the roots over the cone, and gently piled on the soil we'd just removed, making sure the rose was at its original planting level. We watered each rose, let the water seep into the dirt, watered again, and called the operation finished.

Kevin grabbed a rake and started working on the leaves that had fallen into the front flower beds. I followed behind him, pulling the last of the year's weeds. When he headed into the backyard to rake his vegetable beds, I stayed in front to plant bulbs and lily-of-the-valley, put in ornamental cabbage and dusty miller, and deadhead the pansies one last time.

I dug shallow holes around the clerodendrum and plugged in tiny crocus bulbs. In another part of the same border, I tossed tulip and dwarf iris bulbs and dug the holes where the bulbs fell. Daffodils and hyacinths went into the bed that ran beneath the battered azalea border. I tossed, and dug, and hoped that the next spring would finally bring that massed-together look that I'd been trying to achieve.

"Do you think we should mulch the roses?" Kevin asked as I returned my hand fork to the garage.

"Mulch? What made you think of mulch? We've never mulched anything before."

"My mom used to mulch her roses every fall. I'll bet they need some protection after being moved."

I shrugged. "Whatever. Let's look in the garden books."

We looked. We mulched. A quick trip to the nursery netted us two large bags of finely shredded, deep, dark bark dust. As I paid for the mulch, Kevin was busy studying the bulletin board near the door. "Look!" he said. "We can get a truckload of the stuff really cheap."

"We don't need a truckload," I said, tugging at the handle of the wagon.

"Maybe I should mulch my fruit trees." Kevin tore off a slip of paper that had the mulch supplier's phone number on it.

"We'll probably have enough left over for your trees when we're done with the roses." We headed out the door.

"But it would be so much less expensive to buy it in bulk!"

"But, Kevin, we don't need to mulch that much. Here, help me with this, will ya?" We threw the heavy bags into the trunk of the car and returned the wagon.

"Maybe we could get Mary to split a truckload with us."

"Okay. You ask her."

Kevin started the car and we headed home.

Our two bags of mulch proved plenty for the roses and the fruit trees. We could have used another bag for the rhododendrons, but decided against it. A truckload was definitely out; we couldn't find anyone who wanted to split it with us.

One soggy November Saturday, Keith's nephew showed up with two helpers to dig the holes for our two new trees. (A tree's planting hole should be a few inches deeper than the root ball, and twice as wide. Then you backfill the hole so the tree sits at its original growing level. This may seem redundant, but by digging the hole deeper than the root ball, then replacing the dirt, you break up the soil enough to make easy passage for the roots as they settle in.)

After the holes were ready, the planting crew headed out to Big Trees Today. When they came back, they rolled each tree from the back of the truck down a plank and onto the parking strip, then rolled the root ball into the planting hole. Kevin and I stood in different spots in the yard and shouted directions as they straightened the trees. It was like putting up a Christmas tree but with more at stake. The final step was to water the trees with a mild root-stimulant solution. A little bit of this mixture was left over, and I poured it on the clerodendrum. Hope springs eternal.

Kevin wrote a check, Keith's nephew and his crew drove off, and we stood on the sidewalk admiring our new trees. The maple stood directly in front of the living room windows, where its branches would at least partly block the view of the houses across the street. The flowering plum was opposite my office windows. Both trees looked strong and healthy.

I hugged Kevin. "Thanks for the maple tree."

He hugged me back. "Thanks for the plum tree." After a slight pause, he said, "I wonder if we should mulch them?"

Chapter 12

Blame the Lilies on My Sister

That winter was uncharacteristically severe. We kept a close eye on the battered azalea hedge and the new trees, anxious about their health as cold east winds whipped unchecked down Alder Street.

Elizabeth married at Christmas and moved to Canada. This left me as the only DesCamp sister in Portland, a situation with which I was not pleased. I loved my brothers, and I loved my parents, but I *needed* my sisters.

I coughed and sneezed and complained my way through the cold and dark and rain of January. Kevin worried about the new trees being damaged by the cold and wind. An ugly ice storm hit in late January, taking one maple branch with it. But by early February, the worst of the winter was over.

One Saturday morning, I dug up the clerodendrum and poked around in the dirt beneath it. Sure enough, it was solid clay. The tree's roots looked healthy, as far as I could tell: They were firm, with little rootlets along each main root. I put the tree on the sidewalk and got to work.

First I dug in an entire bag of planting mix, followed by several handfuls of rock phosphate. It took a good twenty minutes of digging before the heavy clay chunks broke into small bits. I piled some of the newly dug dirt outside the hole, put the tree on top of the rest of the dirt, and filled it in. Then I finished off with some root stimulant and stood back. "Okay, little tree, be happy. We have to show Kevin just how wonderful you can be. Therese, too." The thought of her tree outperforming mine still rankled.

During the next few weeks, the plum took on a slight glow. In early March, we woke up to find it had burst into bloom overnight. Each branch carried modest sprays of soft pink flowers, fluffy and lightly fragrant.

"See, isn't it pretty?" Kevin asked. I had to agree.

A week later, during spring break, we awakened to a house-rattling earthquake. Terrified, I jumped out of bed and stood in the bedroom doorway. Kevin stayed under the covers. "I thought we left this stuff behind in San Francisco," I complained when it was over. "I've already been through one Big One."

"Hmmm." Kevin was asleep again almost immediately.

The Spring Break Quake, as it was called, moved our front porch steps four inches away from the porch foundation. But it did nothing to disrupt the unfolding spring flowers. The azaleas, undaunted by both earthquakes and maple branch assaults, put on a hot-pink show that was only slightly marred by the tattered branches. The lilac and the rhododendrons followed with bright colors and, in the case of the lilac, wonderful, memory-laden scents. The bulbs still weren't as close together as I wanted, but they were getting there. They also didn't look as mud bound as they had the previous year. It was obvious, however, that getting a really big show of bloom would take me hundreds of bulbs and hundreds of dollars. I was years away from attaining that goal.

The clerodendrum didn't look too excited about the arrival of spring, but it did unfold some healthy leaves. I convinced myself that there were more leaves, and that they were bigger and greener, than ever before. Meanwhile, my lily-of-the-valley were becoming the clerodendrum of the flower world. For the second year in a row, they were no-shows. Once again, I planted annuals where the lily-of-the-valley had declined to come up.

The two transplanted roses survived the winter with no problems. They sprouted blossoms earlier than the other roses (except, of course, for Cecile, who continued to outperform everything else in the yard), had fewer aphid episodes, and had almost no black spot. The roses in the original bed perked up a little bit, too. They got more sunlight now that the huge maples were gone. None of our roses would win any Rose Festival contests, but they looked healthy and put out pretty, fragrant blossoms.

Almost against my will, I began reading about rose care. I just couldn't help myself, sort of like driving past a really bad car accident and not being able to look away. I devoured information about pruning and planting and black spot and mildew. I bought an issue of *Organic*

Gardening magazine that had an article on rose care. I even caught myself clipping articles from the newspaper for future reference— articles about rose care and classic roses and new roses and blue roses and climbing roses. Of course, I admitted none of this to Kevin.

In the backyard, Kevin's apple and pear trees put out dainty, sweet-smelling blossoms. The honeysuckle and clematis got on with the business of growing farther up and along the side fence. I sowed another packet of scarlet runner beans and added a sweet autumn clematis against the back fence. The strawberries awoke, set blossom, and produced an early crop.

It looked as if the garden would have a good year. I planted two honeysuckle, one in each of the hollow maple stumps, and another clematis underneath the lilac, twining its vines up through the shrub's branches.

We concentrated on the inside of the house that summer, finally ripping out the paint-spotted kitchen carpet, painting the upstairs rooms, having the porch steps rebuilt and the exterior trim touched up. The rest of our spare time was spent bike riding and hanging out in the hammock. Weed patrol, aphid killing, and slug tossing occupied a small part of my time early each morning, giving me a chance to wander around and enjoy all the flowers. I really enjoyed starting each day in the garden. The azalea hedge put out enough new growth to close some of the gaps. We went an entire summer without having one argument about tearing out the clerodendrum, mostly because Kevin was so pleased with how well the transplanted roses were doing.

One July morning I cut rose blossoms from Cecile and the two transplants. The blooms were soft and fragrant, the leaves almost totally free of bugs and spots. Maybe, I mused, my gardening success wasn't due solely to a combination of dumb luck and a relatively mild climate. Maybe, on some level, I had a knack for this gardening stuff.

A thorn stuck through my glove and brought me back to reality.

"Easy to grow? Whoever told you that must be on drugs. I mean, check this thing out." I nodded at the tall, bright pink, exotic-looking lily my sister Jeanne was trying to thrust into my unwilling hands. "It'll never survive in my garden. Especially planting it now. It's July, it's blistering hot, and this thing is in full bloom."

Jeanne ignored me and walked over to the southwest corner of the yard. "It should go right here. There's plenty of sun, and this looks like good soil. Plus, that way the fragrance will blend with the roses and the honeysuckle. And you need a jolt of strong color in that corner. Everything around it is sort of subdued—green and white and soft pink." She put the Stargazer lily down in the garden bed and stood back to admire the effect it made against the green of the azaleas.

Jeanne is the only family member who's not a West Coast resident. And despite living in northern Wisconsin, where winter temperatures regularly plunge well below zero and stay there for weeks at a time, where the summer heat and humidity breed mosquitoes the size of beer tankards, Jeanne has the family gardening gene. She also possesses that charming DesCamp willingness to speak her mind, particularly when it comes to telling her youngest sister what to do.

I glared at her. She smiled sweetly.

"Just grow it for me," she said. "You can't kill them off as long as they have good drainage."

"Jeanne, this is *Portland*. It's the bad-drainage capital of the world. Do you have any idea how many hours I've spent out here digging stuff into this dirt so my plants won't rot?"

"Which means it's probably in great shape right now. Oh, come on. I've got some of these in my garden, so I bought one each for you, Elizabeth, and Therese. Therese has a little window box in Berkeley, and Elizabeth is going to put hers in the front yard in Calgary. And if you plant this one, then when I'm back home I can think of all four of us growing flowers together, and when you look at it you can remember your poor sister stuck in the frozen north." She smiled again and batted her long black eyelashes at me. "Besides, they're really easy."

Alarms went off in my head. I gestured at the clerodendrum, which was better than it had ever been before, but to the uneducated eye undoubtedly looked like a short, not particularly interesting shrub. "See that? That's Therese's idea of easy. If this lily dies an ugly death, you'd better be ready to take the blame."

"Oh, come on, Meg. This is Oregon, home of the modern lily. I can't believe you don't have some already."

"What on earth are you talking about?"

"Lilies. Oregon. In about 1930 some guy named de Graaff moved here from Holland and started trying to develop a lily that would grow in a garden. Before that, lilies only grew in the wild. Nobody could get them to survive in gardens. So de Graaff worked for years right here in the Willamette Valley to hybridize lilies that were disease resistant and hardy and . . ."

"Uh-huh. You're making this up, aren't you? This is like when you guys used to tell me I was adopted."

Jeanne laughed. "No, it's all true. The guy at the nursery told me. Really, modern lilies were pretty much born here. There's no reason you can't grow them in your garden."

"Hmmphh." I looked at the lily, then back at my sister. She smiled again. I sighed, knowing when I'd been bested.

The next morning, I got out my hand fork and dug a hole in the garden bed right where Jeanne had placed the lily. She had, of course, picked the perfect spot. Despite my complaints about the soil, it was in pretty good shape. The lily would have decent drainage and plenty of sunlight. I grudgingly dug in some compost and bone meal and flowering plant food, gently spread the lily's roots out, put it in the ground at its original growing level, covered the roots with dirt, took a long sniff of the heavy fragrance, watered it, and decided to let nature take over.

Four weeks later, I was a converted lily lover. On the strength of that initial planting and regular watering, the lily bloomed throughout August. It made me feel ashamed of myself for resisting its charms, and generously repaid my bad attitude with heavily scented flowers that lasted for weeks on the plant and nearly as long indoors. People walking down the street stopped to ask about the wonderful fragrance. I added lilies to my mental list of bulbs to buy for autumn planting.

In October, I went to Portland Nursery with a list stuffed in the back pocket of my jeans. *Hyacinth: purple, pink. Lily-of-the-valley. Iris, dwarf: deep blue ONLY. Tulips: lipstick red, yellow. Daffodil: white? more yellow. Bulb food. LILIES.*

I hauled a little red wagon from one bulb section to another, loading up on the colors and flowers I wanted, bumping into other gardeners anxious to get their fall planting started. Then I entered the lily aisle. Bright pictures on the front of each box promised gorgeous blooms and fragrant breezes. I found myself reaching for bulbs and then pulling back. I simply couldn't make up my mind.

Three years before, I'd bought spring bulbs in a frenzy, driven home and tossed them into the ground. That had worked, sort of, but now I wanted to plan more thoroughly. I wanted the lilies to work together, to make a statement about color and form and symmetry.

The only problem was, I had no clue what that statement should be.

I stood in the aisle for several minutes, not wanting to leave without any lilies but feeling too overwhelmed to make any decisions. Eventually, three fat Stargazer bulbs made it into my brown paper bag. Stargazers were safe. Stargazers were easy. If nothing else, I knew I could grow them successfully, and they would match, not clash, with my single lily.

On my way to the checkout counter, I passed the information desk. *What the heck,* I thought, and stepped up to the counter just as one of the two employees dispensing advice put down a phone and looked up expectantly.

"Hi. Lilies," I said.

"Okay. What do you need to know?" The woman looked slightly amused.

"That's what I'm wondering. What do I need to know, say, if I want to put a whole bunch of them in one corner of the garden? I've got a single Stargazer right now, and it was beautiful this summer, but what about a whole patch of lilies? What do I have to do to the dirt? And aren't lilies an awful lot of work? I mean, they look so exotic."

The woman smiled. "It's actually pretty easy. The most important thing is to amend your soil really, really well, because they need good drainage. Use one of the planting composts or some mushroom compost and dig it in deep. Then, when you put in the bulbs, add bone meal and some bulb food."

"That's it?"

"Pretty much. You'll want to fertilize when you put the bulbs in, when the shoots start coming up in the spring, and then again right before they bloom. And that's about it."

"Really? Wow. So how close together can I put them? I'd like it to look bright and showy and sort of crowded. Is that okay?"

"Yeah. What I've done is plant a grouping of about a dozen bulbs maybe three to four inches apart. They need some space so that they get good air circulation, otherwise they might get a fungus. And then, if you want to add a ground cover, you could do one of the thymes or a catnip or baby's breath." The phone started ringing. "Excuse me. Hello, Portland Nursery. Can you hold for a moment?" She punched a button, and, cradling the phone under her chin, looked back at me.

Ugh. Definitely not baby's breath. "My cats would destroy everything around if I put in catnip."

"We carry a lot of the catnips that are less fragrant than the *nepeta cataria*, and they're prettier, too."

"Okay, so prep the soil, fertilize three times, don't get them too crowded. And that's it?"

"That's it. Have fun." The woman smiled and punched the phone button. "Hi. What can I help you with?"

So Jeanne was actually right and they're easy, I mused as I stood in line at the checkout. While the people ahead of me paid for their wagonloads of plants and bulbs, I fantasized about putting together a really spectacular lily patch. First, I'd choose the perfect spot—maybe exactly where the sole lily was right now—and dig like crazy. Then I would settle down with my garden books and read everything I could find about lilies. Maybe I'd even get a book about growing lilies. Next I'd figure out which lilies would look best together, make a list, buy them, and plant them.

I've never been organized about anything, least of all gardening. But perhaps this was the start of a whole new me. If I planned ahead for the whole garden, not just the lilies, I could probably cut down on the amount of time I spent crawling around in the dirt. That would translate into more time for biking and hanging out in the hammock. It would also mean fewer bare spots in the dirt, fewer short plants growing behind tall ones, fewer bugs, maybe even less money spent on insecticidal soap.

Planning, research, organization, execution. Suddenly I felt the need for serious couch time with a chocolate chip cookie and a good book. I'd get organized one of these days. But not just yet.

Chapter 13

Oh, Right, Now You Bloom

Another rainy Portland winter arrived and, as usual, my spirits plummeted in direct proportion to the amount of sunshine I saw. An impressive cough left from another bout of bronchitis persisted for nearly two months. I moped around the house in my sweats and drank bottomless cups of tea laced with lemon and honey. I took hot baths. I took drugs. My running shoes sat unused, and I couldn't remember the last time I'd walked over to the Hawthorne Starbucks for a mocha. For weeks, a cloud of Vicks VapoRub emanated from my skin. Nothing helped. *We never should have come to this godforsaken climate*, I thought at least once a day. *I gotta get outta here.*

"Maybe we should take a quick trip somewhere warm and dry," I said one Sunday, glancing hopefully at Kevin over the top of the newspaper's travel section.

Three weeks later, we got off a plane in Palm Springs. Ten glorious days stretched in front of us. We hiked, and lounged by the pool, and drank beer and margaritas at outdoor cafes. We ate heaps of Mexican food. We were, as Kevin said half mockingly more than once, happy Americans enjoying life. By the time our ten days were up, both my cough and my melancholy had disappeared.

And so we entered our fourth spring on Southeast Alder Street.

A lot had changed in our lives. Kevin had taken a job with a startup software firm. His work was fun and interesting, but required a nasty commute from our neighborhood to Portland's westside suburbs. The days of his arriving home at five-thirty were gone. We managed to get in some evening bike rides that spring, but not nearly as many as in years past.

My work had changed as well. I'd given up trying to make a living off the national magazine market and was building my practice by concentrating on local companies and publications. I was also contributing a biweekly commentary to a regional radio news program based in Seattle. It was the most fun I'd ever had with my writing, as I told my sisters during one of our keep-in-touch conference calls. "And I'm working on a play, too, about three sisters who . . ."

"*Three* sisters?" they shrieked in perfect chorus. "Who died?"

I tried to convince them that not everything I wrote came directly from my own life. They didn't believe me.

Late that spring, Bruce from next door moved to Idaho to live with his father. "Just to take a break from being in Portland," he said when he left. I missed him: the opera pouring out of the broken screen door, the sarcastic remarks about my gardening, the amused twitch of his lips when I came out with a phrase he considered particularly Midwestern. I didn't miss the cigarette butts on the sidewalk, or Hoffmann chasing our cats.

Bruce's landlord wasn't particularly concerned about getting the house rented. He came by every week or so and spent a few hours inside the house, cleaning and painting. He told us he couldn't decide whether to rent the house again or sell it. It sat empty for months, awaiting his decision.

During that spring, I vowed to toss slugs for a few minutes each and every morning, rain or shine. In actual practice, this meant I made it into the garden about four times a week, usually right after my morning run. Not quite as good as that Englishman who spent four years doing a nightly slug raid on his garden patch, but pretty good for me.

One warm, dry Saturday afternoon in April, I headed outside to take a slow walk around the front yard. The cats preceded me out the front door. K-word and Whoo took turns dive bombing each other from the top of the birdbath. Pug, concerned as usual with keeping his dignity intact, curled up under our new porch swing and fell asleep in the sun.

I looked around and felt a sense of accomplishment and wonder. Was this actually *my* garden? Had the black thumb of the family really put together such an impressive array of growing, blooming, thriving plants? Daffodils and hyacinths and tulips and irises bloomed in profusion, finally approaching the dense look I'd been trying to achieve for four years. That old standby, sweet alyssum, clustered in fluffy, fragrant mounds around the bulbs. The azalea hedge, continuing to recover from its maple branch encounter, had donned a blazing coat of hot-pink blossoms. The daphne's scent was long gone, but its thick, glossy green leaves added depth to the corner near the lilac, which was close to producing a few armloads of fragrant purple blossoms. The rhododendrons had come through the winter without any ice or cold damage, and were unfolding masses of blossoms. Even the roses looked healthy and ready for a good growing season.

The clerodendrum and the lily-of-the-valley were the sole holdouts. The clerodendrum put out some healthy leaves but not, as far as I could tell, more than the year before. Maybe it still needed a little more time. The lily-of-the-valley were complete no-shows. *I think I have to give up on them,* I told myself. *No sense being ridiculous.*

I walked down to the sidewalk and looked back up at the house. The rock garden, which I'd almost totally ignored, was spectacular with its topping of bright azalea blooms. Violets, sweet alyssum, grape hyacinths, ferns—all things I didn't have to worry about—blossomed in the crevices and peeped out from behind small rocks. Hens and chicks, those fat little green succulents with whirly middles, thrived on the neglect that was their lot in life.

I had to admit it: The yard looked great.

A car pulled up behind me. I turned around and watched as a young woman opened the passenger door, pulled off her shoe, and began wiping what was obviously dog poop off her shoe onto my curb.

For once, I was speechless.

She looked up at me and I found my tongue. "Why are you doing that here?"

"Well, where do you want me to do it?" she replied in the nastiest voice I'd heard in a long time.

I just stared at her and shook my head. She slammed her door and the car roared off just as Kevin walked out the door. "You're not going to believe the latest piece of colorful urban life," I told him.

About an hour later, as I pulled weeds in the azalea border, two people stopped on the sidewalk below. They had Starbucks coffee cups in their hands and big smiles on their faces. "I just want to thank you for this garden," one of them said.

I sat back on my heels and smiled. What a nice change from the dog poop episode. "Thank *you*," I said. "It's a lot of fun." To my surprise, I really meant it.

We'd had other positive remarks on the garden, and I'd noticed people stopping to look at the flowers. I'd also seen more than a few passersby walk right up and boldly snap off a flower or two, which is, I suppose, a sort of bad-mannered compliment. But no one had ever thanked me for the garden before. It was almost as if we were performing some terrific civic duty by growing a garden.

"When we sell this house, it has to be in the spring," I said to Kevin as we sat outside that evening, eating chocolate chip cookies and rocking in the porch swing. Pug sat on my lap, purring as we swung gently back and forth. I had a mug of tea to ward off the late spring chill. Kevin pulled on a UC Berkeley sweatshirt while answering.

"Mmm-hmm," he said, his face emerging from the neck of the sweatshirt. "Why? Do you want to move?"

"No, not really. Except you're so far from work right now. And sometimes I feel really burned out on the urban riff-raff factor. Today, for instance. And it would be fun to have a bigger yard."

"We could move to the westside," Kevin said. "I'd love to be closer to work."

I thought about that for a few moments. "Think we could get a bigger yard on the westside?"

"Yeah, but we'd have a bigger mortgage, too," Kevin said.

My heart thumped. My freelance writing now produced a relatively steady income, but not one that would catapult us into a huge dream house with massive gardening space. "I'd have to get a real job is what you're saying?"

"I'm not saying anything other than that we'd have a bigger mortgage unless we went way out and lived in the suburbs. That would put me really close to work, and we could afford a bigger yard *and* a bigger house. But I know how you feel about the 'burbs."

"Maybe we'll stay here a while longer."

"That's fine with me." Kevin picked up a cookie, inspected it closely for flaws, and ate it in two bites.

I stroked Pug's soft black fur and thought about moving. The cats would probably like having a bigger yard to play in. Maybe it wouldn't be so bad. I mentioned this to Kevin.

"Some people move out of the city for their kids. You'll do it for your cats." He shook his head. "I don't think so, Meg."

"Good. I guess I don't think so either." I moved Pug off my lap and stretched.

"Are you going in already?" Kevin asked.

"No, but there's a patch of weeds near Cecile. I'm going to pull them now so they don't get any funny ideas about staying there."

Kevin shook his head. "I never thought I'd see you pulling weeds at night."

I shrugged. "It's just a few minutes, nothing serious." Then I grinned. "But isn't this a great garden?"

Three days later, I called my parents. "Hi," I said. "We sold our home."

Home selling usually involves a whole list of things most people would rather not think about, starting with worrying about your home's curb appeal and ending with the agony of, if you're lucky, watching strangers tromp through your house and make rude remarks about your furniture and choice of paint colors, and if you're unlucky, throwing an open house that no one attends so you end up feeling like you've been stood up on the night of the junior prom.

I am almost ashamed to admit we went through none of this. Our home sale may have been the easiest, least complicated real estate transaction in the history of Portland.

It all started when Connie, the cellist, told us that her neighbors were trying to buy a home but couldn't find anything they liked. I called them and left a message. They called back. Three minutes later, while I was frantically sweeping cat hair off the floor, the home hunters arrived at our front door with their real estate agent in tow.

"We're thinking about selling, but we're just *thinking* about it," I said as they came in the door with a gleam in their eyes. "We haven't decided for sure. The house isn't on the market. Plus it's a mess." I gestured to the broom I was holding.

"It looks fine," they said in unison. "And the garden!" said the woman. "It's just wonderful."

After a quick walk-through of the house, they went home, then called us with a verbal offer. Thirty minutes later, their agent brought over a written offer.

We were floored. Our emotions ranged from harebrained excitement ("Oh, good God! *How* much money will that give us for a down payment on another house?") to hardheaded practicality ("Look, it's just not supposed to be this easy to sell a house. We'd be nuts to turn it down").

"Okay, we'll write it into the contract that we can take the fruit trees with us," Kevin said as we read and reread the offer and stared at each other across the dining room table. "I wonder if I could move the compost heaps?"

"And I want to come back for my stargazer bulbs this fall. And the hollow maple trunks. And the lilac and daphne. And the tulips." I was starting to feel frantic, so I took a deep breath. "No, no, wait. I think daphne is kind of hard to transplant. And we can get another lilac. The vines will have to stay, of course. The roses can definitely stay." I sighed. So much work, so much love had gone into this first home. Would we ever find anything comparable? "I hope we're doing the right thing."

"I hope so, too." Kevin reached over and took my hand. We sat there, silent, for a few minutes.

"As long as we have to move, shall we look on the westside near my office?" he asked.

"We could do that." I gulped.

"Okay, let's go for it. It's probably the right thing to do."

In the weeks that followed, we were convinced more than once that we had done the wrong thing. One Sunday afternoon spent touring subdivisions near Kevin's office was memorably painful. In less than an hour I was ready to tear up our sales contract and stay forever on Southeast Alder Street.

The next day, we restarted our home search with a focus on an area we knew and loved—Portland's inner eastside. The house we finally ended up with was advertised as having "Your own private grotto!" I'd always thought a grotto was a quiet, wooded spot for prayer and meditation. Our grotto turned out to be a huge, hand-built rock pile, complete with waterfall, that backed up against two corners of the backyard. The water fell from a succession of upper pools nearly ten feet off the ground into a two-foot-deep pool sunk into the garden. All it was missing was a statue of a satyr and some naked nymphs. We promptly dubbed it "The Monstrosity" and made plans to tear it down immediately, if not sooner, and replace it with a fruit tree.

Granted, The Monstrosity was not without its own peculiar attractiveness. It was built of soft gray Columbia River basalt and was thickly planted all along its sides and across the top. On closer inspection, I found a miniature rose bush, a dwarf azalea, some irises riding up on the very top of the structure, a small conifer (which would look suitably tacky covered with little Christmas lights during the holiday season), some flowering plants I couldn't identify, and about a dozen different ferns. Glossy green ivy tumbled over the fence that rose behind The Monstrosity.

"I can put the compost heap here," Kevin said, gesturing to a narrow space between the back of the garage and the fence that ran along the edge of the property.

"And I can put a lilac right there." I pointed to a spot just outside one of the two back doors.

Kevin made a face. "Look how much sun that gets. Plus it's right up against the house. It's the perfect spot for tomatoes."

I made a face back at him. "Whatever. Look! Lily-of-the-valley!"

We continued our outdoor tour. The side and front garden beds had some plants—gladiolus, bleeding heart, *roses, yuk*—but it looked as if the dirt hadn't been fed in years. Two spindly maples languished in the parking strip.

"There's an awful lot to do out here," Kevin said.

"I know," I said, smiling. "So let's do it, hey?"

Despite some cosmetic flaws, the house had good bones. The rooms were generously sized, the hardwood floors in decent shape. The windows, in particular, were stunning. The house would be filled with light even on the darkest days—an important consideration in rain-soaked Portland.

In the weeks between the time we decided to buy the house and the time we actually moved in, Kevin and I did several drive-by waterings of the maples. Late in the evening, we'd pull big jugs of water laced with root stimulant out of the trunk, and, as quietly as possible, sneak over to the wilting trees and soak them. But we couldn't get them to perk up. We ended up donating the maples to Friends of

Trees, an urban tree-planting group, who thought they might be able to revive them. We then made another trip to Big Trees Today. The two tall, well-developed maples we picked out were guaranteed to put on a good show in the fall. This time, Kevin didn't even mention flowering plums, and I didn't remind him.

"It's a nice home," Therese said during one of her visits home from Berkeley. We hadn't moved in yet, but I was taking her on a stealthy tour of the outside of the house. She dug a foot into one of the front garden beds. "Needs work. Manure. Compost. Some rock phosphate. Limes, too, probably."

"Lime," I said automatically, then caught the sly smile on her face. "Jerk." We both laughed.

Kevin, the cats, and I left the little blue house on Alder Street for the last time during a blistering hot July Fourth weekend. I looked back wistfully at the garden when we pulled out of the driveway. I'd been so busy during June that I'd neglected to do much besides water the plants. Weeds were showing up in the garden beds. "I hope they're good to the garden," I said to Kevin.

He reached over and patted my hand.

I spent most of that summer with a paintbrush in my hand. But I had plans, big plans, for that fall. I toured the garden beds with a critical eye, making mental notes of what to take out, what to put in, what to leave alone. In September, I dug in vast amounts of compost and steer manure and rock phosphate and lime. I prepared a lily bed. Our next-door neighbors had a huge clerodendrum, and the fragrance of some late-opening blossoms drifted over into our yard as I worked.

In late September, I made one last trip to Alder Street.

The first thing I saw when I got out of the car was my clerodendrum. It looked two feet taller than when we'd moved out and was covered with tiny, shiny aqua-colored fruit surrounded by petal-like sepals of a shocking scarlet-purple. Most of the white blossoms had dropped into the garden bed, taking with them their fragrance, but the tree still looked stunning.

"Ingrate!" I muttered. "After all I did for you, you waited until I left." Still, I couldn't resist a smile. All along, I'd thought Kevin was telepathically injuring the tree. Now I had proof.

I looked longingly at the little blue house. We'd had such a good life here.

But I had a new garden waiting for me. There were new plants to buy, new mistakes to make, new slugs to toss.

Thirty minutes later, I put my freshly dug lily bulbs and my dirt-covered tools in the back of The Fleshy One and drove home.

Acknowledgments

Where to start? Probably with my mother and father, Jean and Bayard DesCamp, for giving me an early love of books. Mom, thanks for saving everything I wrote, including that autobiography I penned at age six. Dad, I treasure the memories of our post-dinner walks to the library and the bookstore. John, Mike, Ed, Jeanne, Elizabeth, Therese, and Mark: You all had a huge impact on me and, by extension, on this book.

Thanks also to Susan Stanley, for her gentle but persistent kicks in the behind. To Carol Hills, for helping me find my radio voice. To Marie Deatherage, for great laughs and good editing suggestions. To the always helpful staff at Portland Nursery. Any technical mistakes, particularly those involving scary chemicals, are completely my own.

Michelle Decker, Laurie Weigel, Ellie Rickett, Jill Irvin: Without you, I would be completely insane, instead of just partway there.

Special thanks to Gary Luke, for his superb editing skills and life-saving sense of humor.

Finally, to Julia, for being such a fantastic, cheerful child and for napping with such enthusiasm, and most especially to Kevin Renner, the world's best husband, for supporting me in all possible ways during all these years of writing.